NANCY JOHNSON-SREBRO

block magic, too!

Over 50 NEW Blocks from Squares and Rectangles

C&T PUBLISHING

© 2003 Silver Star, Inc.
Editor-in-Chief: Darra Williamson
Editor: Liz Aneloski
Technical Editor: Sara Kate MacFarland
Copyeditor: Linda Smith
Proofreader: Carol Barrett
Cover Designer: Aliza Shalit
Design Director: Aliza Shalit, AK Design
Book Designer: Aliza Shalit, AK Design
Illustrator: Kandy Petersen
Production Assistant: Tim Manibusan
Block Photography: Diane Pedersen
Quilt Photography: Sharon Risedorph
Published by C&T Publishing, Inc.,
P.O. Box 1456, Lafayette, California 94549

Back cover: *Into the Woods*, made by Maryjane Simpson
and quilted by Leslie Armando.

Library of Congress Cataloging-in-Publication Data
Johnson-Srebro, Nancy.
  Block magic, too! : over 50 new blocks from squares and rectangles /
Nancy Johnson-Srebro.
      p. cm.
  ISBN 1-57120-191-2
  1. Patchwork—Patterns. 2. Quilting—Patterns. 3. Patchwork quilts.
I. Title.
  TT835 .J5865 2003
  746.46'041—dc21
                                    2002011877

Printed in China

10   9   8   7   6   5   4   3   2   1

table of contents

dedication

This book is dedicated to our children; Mark, Alan, and Karen.
Each of you in your own way has enriched my life.

acknowledgments

A heartfelt thank you is extended to the following people:

Cindy Cochran, Janet McCarroll, Arlene Shea, Maryjane Simpson, and C. A. Warner-Bradigan, for the super job of proofing patterns and sewing hundreds of samples;

Our daughter-in-law, Jennifer, special thanks for designing several patterns;

Lea Wang from Custom Machine Quilting, NJ, for her wonderful machine quilting skills;

Georgia Adamitis, Karen Bolesta, Karen Brown, Vicki Novajosky, Ellen Pahl, Marcia Rickansrud and Roxanne Sidorek, for their friendship and constant support;

Liz Aneloski and Sara MacFarland, my very talented editors; also, Todd Hensley and the rest of the staff at C&T. The kindness you showed me throughout this project is greatly appreciated;

American & Efird, Benartex, Inc., Bernina of America, Fairfield Processing Corporation, FreeSpirit, Just Another Button Company, Stearns Technical Textiles, P&B Textiles, Prym Dritz/Omnigrid, RJR Fashion Fabrics, Robert Kaufman Co., Inc, Timeless Treasures, and The Warm Company.

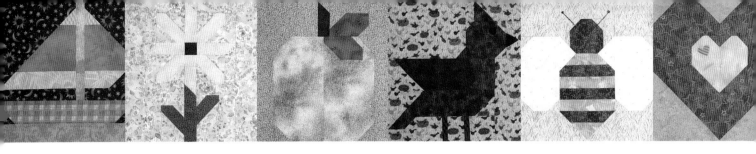

INTRODUCTION

I have little self-control when it comes to quilting. Just ask my husband, family, friends, and quilters I've taught or talked with. The quilters will understand what I'm talking about but I'm not sure my family does. In 2001 I finished *Block Magic*, and I promised my family and myself I would take some time off. I don't know what happened! Maybe it was the excitement that was created by *Block Magic*. We received many letters and calls asking for another book containing more original patterns with No-Fail® methods. The next thing I knew I had dug out the graph paper, was

drawing lines and shapes, and had over fifty new patterns designed! And, as before, each pattern only required cutting SQUARES and RECTANGLES! It doesn't get any better than that.

Whatever the reasons, I hope you get a ton of pleasure from this book. Relax and let your imagination take you to new quilting heights.

Now, I've promised my family I would take some time off after this book. . . . We'll see. Enjoy!

how to read the charts

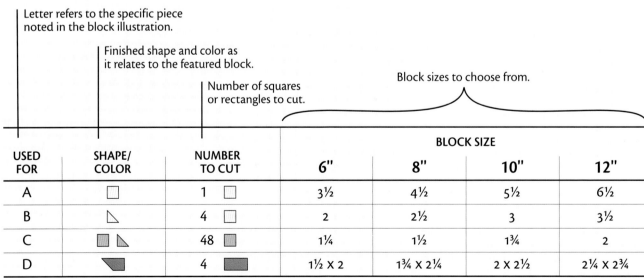

Letter refers to the specific piece noted in the block illustration.

Finished shape and color as it relates to the featured block.

Number of squares or rectangles to cut.

Block sizes to choose from.

USED FOR	SHAPE/ COLOR	NUMBER TO CUT	BLOCK SIZE			
			6"	8"	10"	12"
A	☐	1 ☐	3½	4½	5½	6½
B	◺	4 ☐	2	2½	3	3½
C	☐ ◺	48 ☐	1¼	1½	1¾	2
D	▱	4 ▭	1½ X 2	1¾ X 2¼	2 X 2½	2¼ X 2¾

Measurements are given in inches.
Single measurements indicate the size of a cut square (2 = 2" x 2").

THE BASICS

ROTARY CUTTING EQUIPMENT

The quality of the equipment used for piecing and quilt-making makes the difference in how good the finished quilt will look. Use accurately printed rulers along with a good-quality cutting mat, such as Omnigrid rulers and mats. For added cutting ease, try using Invisi-Grip on the bottom of your rulers; it will keep the ruler from slipping while cutting on any fabric. Also, be sure to use a rotary cutter that is suited for your personal style and physical needs. I've found that the Omnigrid or Dritz 45mm Pressure-Sensitive rotary cutter allows me to rotary cut for hours without hand fatigue.

ROTARY CUTTING

There are only two geometric shapes used throughout the patterns in this book; a square and a rectangle. Both are very easy to rotary cut. The photographs that follow in this section illustrate both left-handed and right-handed cutting techniques.

Cutting a Square

step one The instructions for the block will show the cut height of a square. This will determine the width of the strip you will cut. For example, if the instructions require four 3" x 3" squares, cut a strip of fabric 3" x 13". Always cut the strip a little longer than necessary; this allows you to "square up" the short end of the strip. Place the short side of the ruler along the top of the strip. Square-up the short side of the strip by cutting approximately ¼" from the edge.

step two After squaring up one end of the strip, turn the mat one-half a turn (180°). Place the ruler on top of the fabric so the 3" marking lines up with the newly cut edge. Be sure the top of the ruler is even with the top of the strip. Rotary cut.

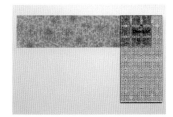 

Left-Handed   Right-Handed

Cutting a Rectangle

step one The instructions for the block will show the cut height of the short side of a rectangle. This will determine the width of the strip you will cut. Let's say the block instructions call for two 3" x 5" rectangles. Cut a strip of fabric 3" x 11", allowing extra length for squaring-up. Square-up the short end of the strip as shown in Step 1 for cutting a square.

step two Turn the mat one-half a turn (180°) and place the ruler on top of the strip so the 5" marking lines up with the newly cut edge. Be sure the top of the ruler is even with the top of the strip. Rotary cut.

 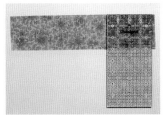 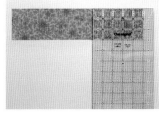 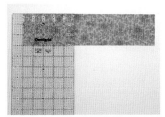

Left-Handed   Right Handed   Left-Handed   Right-Handed

THE BASICS

FABRIC AND THREAD CHOICES

For best results, I encourage you to use good quality 100% cotton fabrics. You can find cottons at quilt shops throughout the world. If possible, prewash the fabrics before using them. This ensures the fabrics are preshrunk and the dyes won't bleed if your block or quilt must be washed in the future.

I do all my machine piecing with Mettler 100% cotton silk finish thread (50/3 weight). For most of my piecing I use a light beige color thread (color #703 or #810). However, when I sew on black fabric, I use navy blue thread, and black thread when I sew on navy blue fabric. The slight difference between the thread and fabric colors is just enough to make it easy to rip out seams if necessary.

SEWING

One of the joys you will discover while sewing the blocks in this book is that it's all straight stitching; no back tacking, no set-in seams, no bias edges to deal with. You may even try some strip piecing if you plan to use the same fabrics and make several identical blocks.

I recommend you lay out all of the block pieces on a small rigid surface like an extra cutting mat before sewing the block together. This enables you to move the block to the sewing machine easily, and reduces sewing errors.

I want to share some special hints and tips to help you build your sewing skills. When you start making original blocks, problems can arise no matter how much you have sewn. Following the suggestions in this section will help you avoid most, if not all, of these.

Seam Allowance

It's best to use a scant ¼" seam allowance when quilt piecing. This scant seam allowance ensures the units/blocks are true to size because it allows for the small amount of fabric that is lost due to the thickness of the sewing thread and the resulting "hump" that's created by pressing the seam allowances to one direction.

Hints for Sewing on the Diagonal

Follow these hints for sewing diagonal seams and get perfect piecing results every time.

1. Some of the squares and rectangles require you to draw a thin pencil line diagonally through the piece in order to sew it to the next piece. DO NOT sew precisely on the drawn pencil line. Sew one or two thread widths to the right of it. This ensures the piece will be the correct size after pressing. If you sew exactly on the pencil line, the piece will likely be too small after pressing.

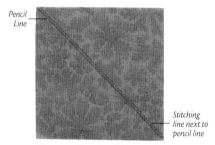

Pencil Line

Stitching line next to pencil line

Stitch just to the right of the pencil line.

2. Use a mechanical pencil with a lead no more than 0.5mm in diameter for drawing the diagonal lines on your fabric. Do not use a regular pencil. It becomes dull very quickly and the pencil line is wider and bolder than desired.

3. Keep sharp needles in your sewing machine. A dull needle will distort the first few stitches. I use a 70/10 Jeans/Denim by Schmetz for all of my machine piecing.

4. A single-hole throat/stitch plate is also helpful. It keeps the needle from pushing the corner of the square into the zigzag throat/stitch plate hole (which has a larger opening).

5. When sewing diagonally through a square or rectangle, start sewing on a scrap piece of fabric first, then sew into the adjacent square/rectangle. This helps prevent distortion of the first one or two stitches.

6. Do your piecing with an open-toe walking foot. This allows you to see where to sew NEXT to the pencil line. I do all of my machine piecing on a Bernina 170 with an open-toe walking foot.

7. The needle-stop down feature on my sewing machine is very helpful when chain piecing. Use this feature if your machine has it.

8. Press the diagonally sewn seam FIRST. This prevents distortion of the seam and pieces. Then trim off the excess fabric.

Sewing on the Diagonal Using a Square and a Rectangle

step one On the wrong side of the fabric, draw a diagonal line across the square. With right sides together, place the square on the rectangle. Stitch one or two thread widths to the right of the pencil line.

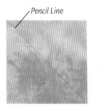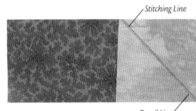

Pencil Line

Stitching Line

Pencil Line

step two Press the square according to the pressing arrows in the block instructions. Carefully lay the pieces on a cutting mat. Using a ruler and rotary cutter, trim ¼" away from the stitching line. You will have a triangle-shaped piece of fabric left over. Discard or save these pieces for future projects. The amount of fabric discarded is well worth the precision and accuracy you gain by using this sewing method.

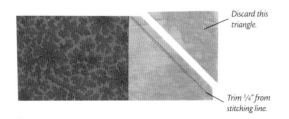

Discard this triangle.

Trim ¼" from stitching line.

Sewing on the Diagonal Using Two Rectangles

step one In order to draw a pencil line on a rectangle, position the top rectangle a little away from the edge of the rectangle that is beneath it. This allows you to see where to draw the diagonal pencil line.

step two Draw a pencil line from the upper corner diagonally to where the rectangles meet (45°). Move the top rectangle so the edges of the two rectangles are even. You are now ready to sew, press, and trim ¼" from the stitching line.

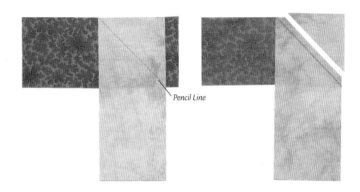

Pencil Line

PRESSING HINTS

1. Be sure to press each seam allowance before you sew more pieces to the unit.

2. I've included pressing arrows in the block instructions. These are only suggestions but are highly recommended. If you follow these pressing arrows, you should be able to butt most of your pieces together, and accurately align and stitch the pieces together. This helps keep your blocks square.

3. Do not press with steam. It tends to distort many of the small pieces.

4. Use the cotton setting on your iron. If this doesn't seem hot enough, set it one notch higher. After pressing a piece, it should lie fairly flat on the ironing board. If it doesn't, it's a sure sign that the iron isn't hot enough.

5. To get stubborn seam allowances to lie flat, place a tiny piece of ¼" wide Steam-a-Seam 2 under the seam allowance and press. This fuses the seam allowance in place.

THE BASICS

EMBELLISHMENT

I didn't plan to do very much embellishing on my blocks, but after seeing the buttons from Just Another Button Company, I became enthusiastic. To make it easy for you, I've given you the template patterns for eyes, noses, wheels, etc. The patterns are sized for the 12" block. Enlarge or reduce proportionally to fit the size of your block. Add the embellishment details after piecing the block. I used a fusible product called Steam-a-Seam 2 by The Warm Company for fusing or machine appliqué. If you want to hand appliqué your pieces instead of fusing them, trace 1/8" from the outside edge of the template. Then turn the edge under 1/8" and hand stitch the pieces in place. Let your imagination go wild!

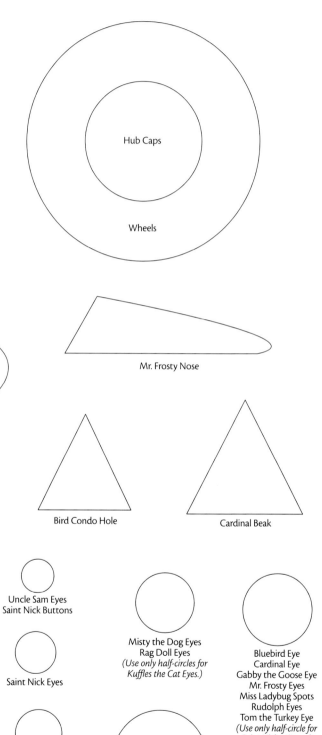

Hub Caps

Wheels

Mr. Frosty Nose

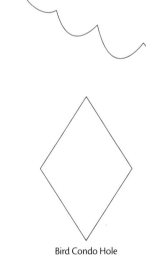

Saint Nick Beard

Bird Condo Hole

Cardinal Beak

Bird Condo Hole

Bird
Condo Hole

Hurricane
Lamp Flame

Uncle Sam Eyes
Saint Nick Buttons

Misty the Dog Eyes
Rag Doll Eyes
*(Use only half-circles for
Kuffles the Cat Eyes.)*

Bluebird Eye
Cardinal Eye
Gabby the Goose Eye
Mr. Frosty Eyes
Miss Ladybug Spots
Rudolph Eyes
Tom the Turkey Eye
*(Use only half-circle for
Saint Nick Mittens.)*

Saint Nick Eyes

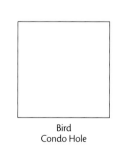

Uncle Sam Mustache
(reverse for other side)

Misty the Dog Nose

Mr. Frosty Mouth
Swimmin' Fish Eyes
*(Use only half-circles for
Kuffles the Cat nose.)*

Bird
Condo Hole

double hearts *(Design by Nancy Johnson-Srebro)*

This block makes a wonderful border; the hearts give a staggered look.

USED FOR	SHAPE/ COLOR	NUMBER TO CUT	BLOCK SIZE				
			4"	6"	8"	10"	12"
A		2	1½ x 2½	2 x 3½	2½ x 4½	3 x 5½	3½ x 6½
B		4	1½	2	2½	3	3½
C		8	⅞	1	1⅛	1⅜	1½
D		4*	1½ x 3½	2 x 5	2½ x 6½	3 x 8	3½ x 9½

*Use two different fabrics for D.

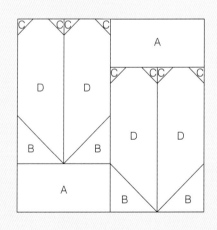

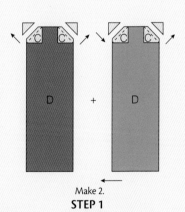

Make 2.
STEP 1

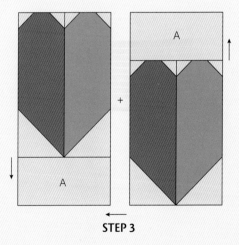

STEP 3

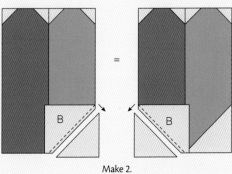

Make 2.
STEP 2

sails a'flying
(Design by Nancy Johnson-Srebro)

Make some very colorful sails and watch the fun begin.

  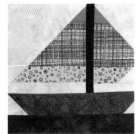

USED FOR	SHAPE/ COLOR	NUMBER TO CUT	BLOCK SIZE			
			6"	8"	10"	12"
A	◺	1 ▢	4¼	5½	6¾	8
B	◹	1 ▭	2⅜ X 2⅝	3 X 3⅜	3⅝ X 4	4¼ X 4¾
C	▭	1 ▭	1 X 4¼	1⅛ X 5½	1⅜ X 6¾	1½ X 8
D	▭	1 ▭	1 X 2⅜	1⅛ X 3	1⅜ X 3⅝	1½ X 4¼
E	◺	1 ▢	1¼	1½	1¾	2
F	◺	1 ▢	1	1⅛	1⅜	1½
G	◺	1 ▢	1½	1⅞	2⅛	2½
H	▬	1 ▬	⅞ X 4¾	1 X 6⅛	1⅛ X 7⅝	1¼ X 9
I	◺	1 ▭	1¼ X 4	1½ X 5⅛	1¾ X 6⅜	2 X 7½
J	◺	1 ▭	1¼ X 2⅜	1½ X 3	1¾ X 3⅝	2 X 4¼
K	◹	1 ▭	2½ X 4	3⅛ X 5⅛	3⅞ X 6⅜	4½ X 7½
L	◹	1 ▭	2⅜ X 2½	3 X 3⅛	3⅝ X 3⅞	4¼ X 4½
M	◢	1 ▭	1¼ X 4	1½ X 5⅛	1¾ X 6⅜	2 X 7½
N	◣	1 ▭	1¼ X 2⅜	1½ X 3	1¾ X 3⅝	2 X 4¼
O	▱	1 ▬	1½ X 6½	1⅞ X 8½	2⅛ X 10½	2½ X 12½
P	▭	1 ▬	1¼ X 6½	1½ X 8½	1¾ X 10½	2 X 12½

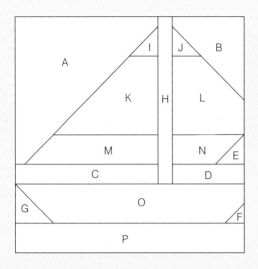

tip

Personalize this block by printing or embroidering your name or initials on the sails or front of the boat.

STEP 1

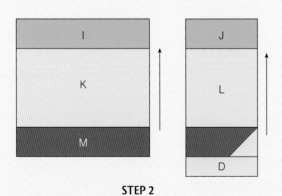

STEP 2

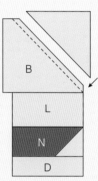

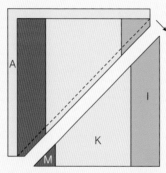

Line up the bottom of I/K/M with the lower right corner of A square.

Line up the top of J with the long side of rectangle B.

STEP 3

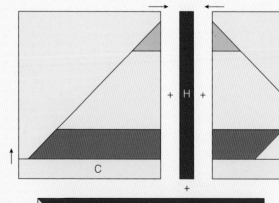

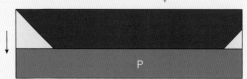

STEP 4

antique bottle and crock

(Design by Nancy Johnson-Srebro)

Try using hand-dyed fabric for the bottle or crock, or both!

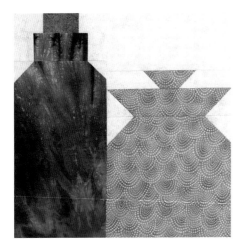

USED FOR	SHAPE/ COLOR	NUMBER TO CUT	BLOCK SIZE			
			6"	8"	10"	12"
A	▭	4 ▭	1 x 1¼	1⅛ x 1½	1⅜ x 1¾	1½ x 2
B	◺	2 ▢	1	1⅛	1⅜	1½
C	▭	1 ▭	2 x 4	2⅝ x 5⅛	2⅞ x 6⅜	3½ x 7½
D	▱ ▱	2 ▭	1 x 2	1⅛ x 2½	1⅜ x 3	1½ x 3½
E	◺	4 ▢	1¼	1½	1¾	2
F	▽	1 ▭	1 x 2	1⅛ x 2⅜	1⅜ x 3⅛	1½ x 3½
G	▽	1 ▭	1¼ x 4	1½ x 5⅛	1¾ x 6⅜	2 x 7½
H	⬔	1 ▭	3¾ x 4	4¾ x 5⅛	6 x 6⅜	7 x 7½
I	▬	1 ▬	1 x 1½	1⅛ x 1⅞	1⅜ x 2⅛	1½ x 2½
J	▬	1 ▬	1¼ x 2	1½ x 2⅝	1¾ x 2⅞	2 x 3½
K	▭	1 ▬	3 x 5¼	3⅞ x 6⅞	4⅝ x 8⅜	5½ x 10

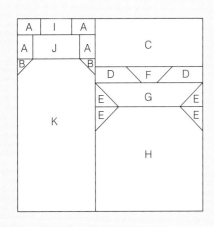

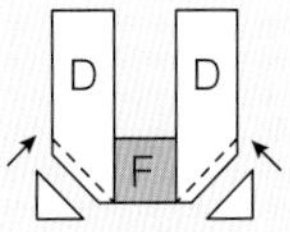

STEP 1

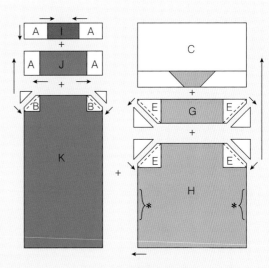

STEP 2

✳short side of rectangle H

angel of the heart

(Design by Nancy Johnson-Srebro)

Whether you make her wings light or dark, this angel will steal your heart! Add embroidered eyelashes to give her a peaceful look.

USED FOR	SHAPE/ COLOR	NUMBER TO CUT	BLOCK SIZE			
			6"	8"	10"	12"
A		2	3⅛	4	4⅞	5¾
B		2	1	1⅛	1⅜	1½
C		2	1¼	1½	1¾	2
D		2	1 x 2½	1⅛ x 3¼	1⅜ x 3¾	1½ x 4½
E		1	1 x 3½	1⅛ x 4½	1⅜ x 5½	1½ x 6½
F		2	1	1⅛	1⅜	1½
G		2	2 x 6½	2½ x 8½	3 x 10½	3½ x 12½
H		4	1½	1¾	2⅛	2½
I		2	1¼	1½	1¾	2
J		1	2½	3¼	3¾	4½
K		1	3½ x 4	4½ x 5⅛	5½ x 6⅜	6½ x 7½

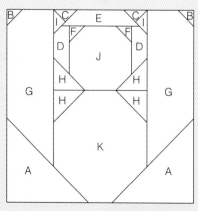

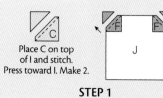

Place C on top of I and stitch. Press toward I. Make 2.

STEP 1

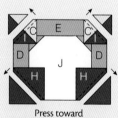

Press toward D and E before adding H and C/I units.

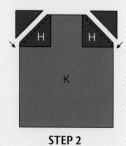

STEP 2

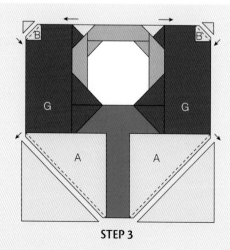

STEP 3

barney the bear

(Design by Nancy Johnson-Srebro)

Dig out your sky and grass fabrics.

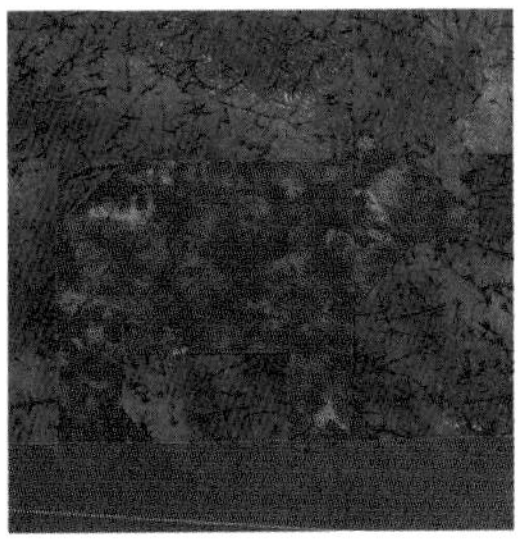

USED FOR	SHAPE/ COLOR	NUMBER TO CUT	BLOCK SIZE			
			6"	8"	10"	12"
A		1	2¼ x 4½	2¾ x 5¾	3½ x 7⅛	4 x 8½
B		1	2¼ x 2½	2¾ x 3¼	3½ x 3⅞	4 x 4½
C		1	¾ x 1	⅞ x 1¼	⅞ x 1¼	1 x 1½
D		1	1 x 1½	1⅛ x 1¾	1¼ x 2	1½ x 2½
E		2	1¼	1½	1¾	2
F		1	¾	¾	¾	1
G		1	2½ x 2¾	3¼ x 3½	3⅞ x 4¼	4½ x 5
H		1	1½ x 2½	1¾ x 3⅛	2 x 3¾	2½ x 4½
I		1	1 x 3¾	1⅛ x 4¾	1⅜ x 5¾	1½ x 7
J		1	2¾ x 4	3½ x 5⅛	4¼ x 6¼	5 x 7½
K		1	1½ x 2	1¾ x 2⅝	2 x 3⅛	2½ x 3½
L		1	¾ x 1	⅞ x 1¼	⅞ x 1¼	1 x 1½
M		2	1¼ x 1½	1½ x 1¾	1¾ x 2	2 x 2½
N		1	1¼	1½	1¾	2
O		2	⅞	1	1⅛	1¼
P		1	1½ x 6½	2 x 8½	2¼ x 10½	2½ x 12½

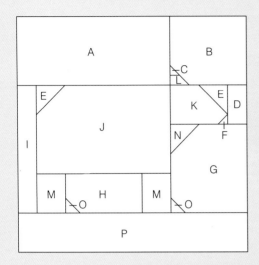

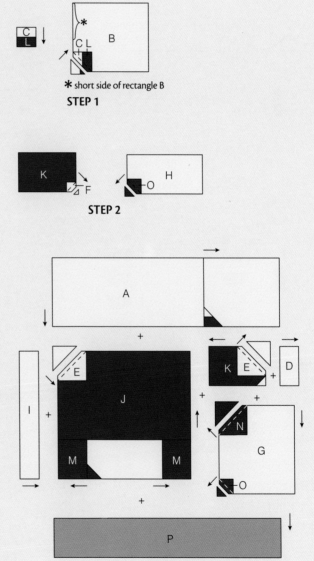

STEP 1

* short side of rectangle B

STEP 2

STEP 3

tip

Make it black, brown, white, or tan. If you are making a polar bear, use fabric that looks like ice crystals for the ground.

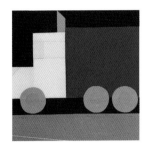

big hauler *(Design by Nancy Johnson-Srebro)*

Watch this truck whiz by when you use striped fabric for the road.

USED FOR	SHAPE/ COLOR	NUMBER TO CUT	BLOCK SIZE			
			6"	8"	10"	12"
A	▭	1	1½ x 2⅝	1¾ x 3¼	2¼ x 4	2½ x 4¾
B	▭	1	1¼ x 4	1½ x 5¼	1¾ x 6⅜	2 x 7½
C	◺	1	⅞	1	1⅛	1¼
D	▭	1	1½ x 2	1¾ x 2½	2⅛ x 3	2½ x 3½
E	▭	1	1¼ x 6½	1½ x 8½	1¾ x 10½	2 x 12½
F	▭	1	1¾ x 6½	2¼ x 8½	2½ x 10½	3 x 12½
G	▭	1	1 x 1¼	1⅛ x 1½	1⅜ x 1¾	1½ x 2
H	◺	1	⅞	1	1⅛	1¼
I	▭	1	⅞ x 2	1 x 2½	1⅛ x 3	1¼ x 3½
J	▭	1	1¼ x 1½	1½ x 1⅞	1¾ x 2⅛	2 x 2½
K	▭	1	2 x 2⅜	2½ x 3	3 x 3⅝	3½ x 4¼
L	▭	1	1½ x 2	1¾ x 2½	2⅛ x 3	2½ x 3½
M	▭	1	3¾ x 4	4¾ x 5¼	6 x 6⅜	7 x 7½
N	◢	1	⅞ x 1½	1 x 1¾	1⅛ x 2¼	1¼ x 2½
Wheels and hubcaps ● ○		3*, 3*	See page 10			

*Fuse on after sewing the complete block.

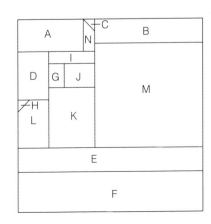

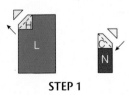

STEP 1

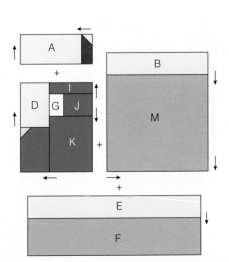

STEP 2

bird condo

(Design by Cindy Mundy Cochran)

What bird wouldn't love to live in this condo?

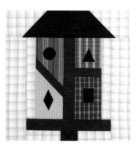

USED FOR	SHAPE/ COLOR	NUMBER TO CUT	BLOCK SIZE			
			6"	8"	10"	12"
A		2	1¾ x 2½	2⅛ x 3¼	2½ x 3⅞	3 x 4½
B		2	1½ x 5¼	2 x 6⅞	2¼ x 8½	2½ x 10
C		2	1 x 4¼	1⅛ x 5⅝	1⅜ x 6¾	1½ x 8
D		2	1 x 2⅛	1⅛ x 2½	1⅜ x 3⅛	1½ x 3¾
E		1	1 x 1¼	1⅛ x 1½	1⅜ x 1¾	1½ x 2
F		1	1¾ x 2¾	2⅛ x 3½	2½ x 4¼	3 x 5
G		1	1¾ x 2¾	2⅛ x 3½	2½ x 4¼	3 x 5
H		1	1¾	2⅛	2½	3
I		1	1¾ x 2⅝	2⅛ x 3½	2½ x 4⅛	3 x 4¾
J		1	1 x 4¼	1 x 5⅝	1¼ x 6¾	1½ x 8
K		1	⅞ x 1¾	1 x 2⅛	1⅛ x 2½	1¼ x 3
L		1	1¾ x 2¼	2⅛ x 2⅞	2½ x 3¼	3 x 4
M		1	1 x 4½	1⅛ x 5½	1⅜ x 7	1½ x 8½
N		1	1¾ x 5	2⅛ x 6¼	2½ x 7¾	3 x 9½
Holes	●▲■◆	1*, 1*, 1*, 1*	See page 10			

*Fuse on after sewing the complete block.

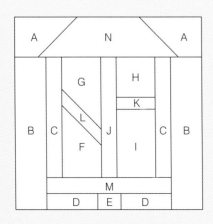

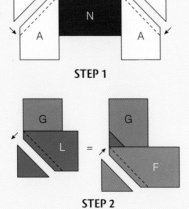

STEP 1

STEP 2

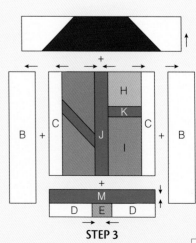

STEP 3

tom the turkey

(Design by Nancy Johnson-Srebro)

Dress up this fellow with all sorts of fancy fabrics.

USED FOR	SHAPE/ COLOR	NUMBER TO CUT	BLOCK SIZE			
			6"	9"	12"	15"
A	⬜	1	1¼ X 1¾	1⅝ X 2⅜	2 X 3	2⅜ X 3⅝
B	⬜	1	1¼ X 4¼	1⅝ X 6⅛	2 X 8	2⅜ X 9⅞
C	◺	12	1	1¼	1½	1¾
D	◺	2	1½ X 4	2 X 5¾	2½ X 7½	3 X 9¼
E	⬜	1	1¼ X 2	2 X 2¾	2½ X 3½	3 X 4¼
F	◺	2	1½	2	2½	3
G	⬜	2	1½ X 2⅝	2 X 3⅝	2½ X 4¾	3 X 5¾
H	⬜	2	1 X 1½	1¼ X 2	1½ X 2½	1¾ X 3
I	◣	2	⅞	1⅛	1¼	1½
J	▭	2	⅞ X 1½	1⅛ X 2	1¼ X 2½	1½ X 3
K	◣	1	1⅛	1⅜	1¾	2
L	⬛	1	2¼ X 3⅝	3⅛ X 5⅛	4 X 6¾	4⅞ X 8⅛
M	◣	1	2¼ X 2⅝	3⅛ X 3¾	4 X 4¾	4⅞ X 6
N	⬛	1	2 X 5	2¾ X 6⅞	3½ X 9	4¼ X 11⅛
O	▽	5	1 X 4	1¼ X 5¾	1½ X 7½	1¾ X 9¼
P	◿◹	5	1 X 4	1¼ X 5¾	1½ X 7½	1¾ X 9¼
Eye	●	1*	See page 10			

*Fuse on after sewing the complete block.

tip

Go wild with the fabrics for the feathers. The more variety the better!

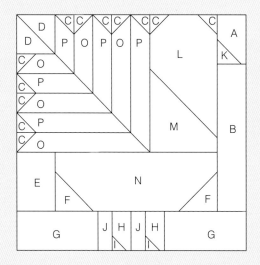

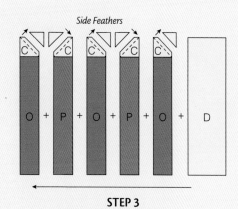

Side Feathers

O + P + O + P + O + D

STEP 3

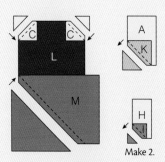

Make 2.

STEP 1

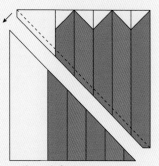

Place side feathers on top of top feathers. Butt seams, stitch, and trim.

STEP 4

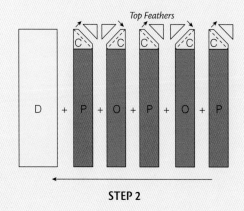

Top Feathers

D + P + O + P + O + P

STEP 2

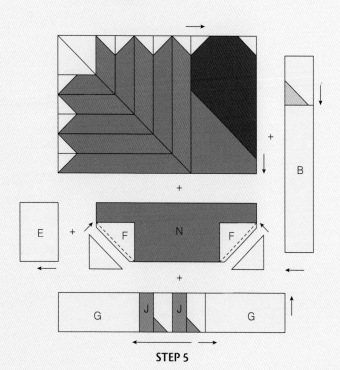

STEP 5

black-eyed susan

(Design by Nancy Johnson-Srebro)

I love these flowers. Sew a bunch and enjoy!

USED FOR	SHAPE/ COLOR	NUMBER TO CUT	BLOCK SIZE			
			6"	9"	12"	15"
A	▭	2 ▭	1½ x 6½	2 x 9½	2½ x 12½	3 x 15½
B	▭	2 ▭	1¼ x 2½	1⅝ x 3½	2 x 4½	2⅜ x 5½
C	▱	1 ▭	1½ x 1¾	2 x 2⅜	2½ x 3	3 x 3⅝
D	▱	1 ▭	1½ x 2¼	2 x 3⅛	2½ x 4	3 x 4⅞
E	▭	1 ▭	1 x 1½	1¼ x 2	1½ x 2½	1¾ x 3
F	◺	5 ▢	1	1¼	1½	1¾
G	▭	4 ▭	1 x 2¼	1¼ x 3⅛	1½ x 4	1¾ x 4⅞
H	▭	4 ▭	1 x 1¾	1¼ x 2⅜	1½ x 3	1¾ x 3⅝
I	◺	8 ▢	1⅜	1⅞	2¼	2¾
J	⬡	4 ▢	1¾	2⅜	3	3⅝
K	▱	4 ▭	1 x 2¼	1¼ x 3⅛	1½ x 4	1¾ x 4⅞
L	■	1 ■	1	1¼	1½	1¾
M	▱	2 ▭	1½ x 1¾	2 x 2⅜	2½ x 3	3 x 3⅝
N	▱	1 ▭	1 x 3	1¼ x 4¼	1½ x 5½	1¾ x 6¾

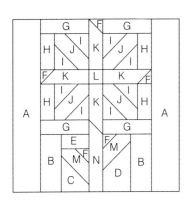

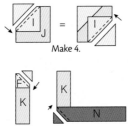

Make 4.

Make 3.

STEP 1

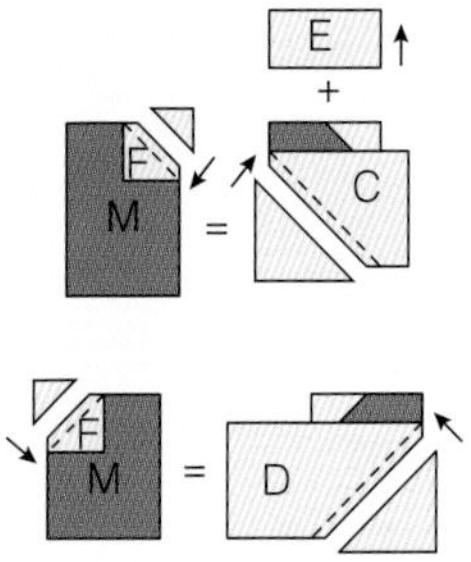

STEP 2

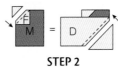

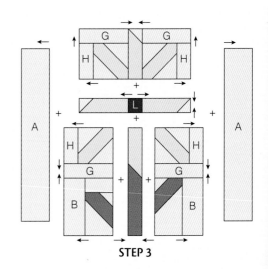

STEP 3

cherry basket

(Design by Nancy Johnson-Srebro)

Fill this basket with fruit or flowers.

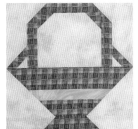

USED FOR	SHAPE/ COLOR	NUMBER TO CUT	BLOCK SIZE			
			6"	8"	10"	12"
A		2	1½ x 3½	1⅞ x 4½	2⅛ x 5½	2½ x 6½
B		2	1½	1¾	2¼	2½
C		2	1	1¼	1¼	1½
D		1	3 x 3½	3⅞ x 4½	4⅝ x 5½	5½ x 6½
E		2	2¾	3½	4¼	5
F		2	1¼ x 2¾	1½ x 3½	1¾ x 4¼	2 x 5
G		1	1¼ x 3½	1½ x 4½	1¾ x 5½	2 x 6½
H		1	1¼ x 6½	1½ x 8½	1¾ x 10½	2 x 12½
I		1	1½ x 6½	1⅞ x 8½	2⅛ x 10½	2½ x 12½
J		2	1½	1⅞	2⅛	2½
K		2	1 x 3	1⅛ x 3⅞	1⅜ x 4⅝	1½ x 5½
L		2	1¼	1½	1¾	2
M		1	1 x 4½	1⅛ x 5¾	1⅜ x 7¼	1½ x 8½
N		1	1 x 6½	1⅛ x 8½	1⅜ x 10½	1½ x 12½

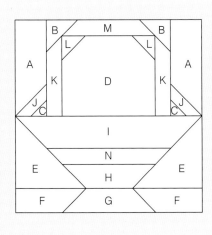

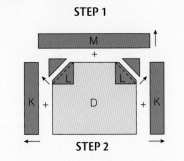

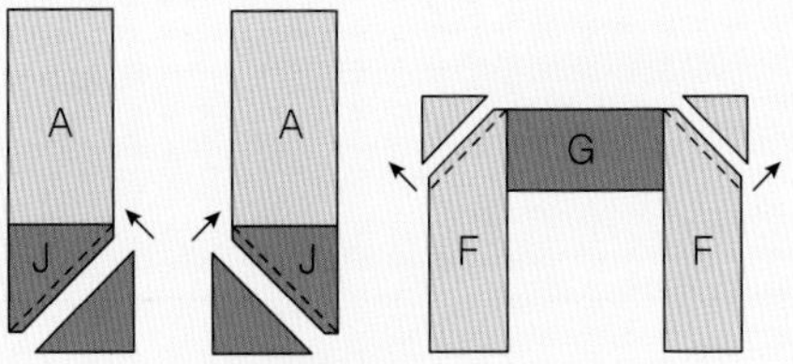

STEP 1

STEP 2

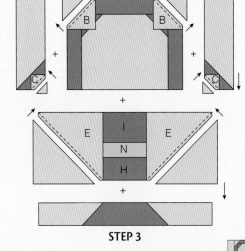

STEP 3

cherry basket

23

bluebird
(Design by Nancy Johnson-Srebro)

You can use different fabrics to make a robin, too!

USED FOR	SHAPE/ COLOR	NUMBER TO CUT	BLOCK SIZE			
			6"	8"	10"	12"
A	▭	1 ▭	1⅝ X 3⅛	2 X 4	2⅜ X 4⅞	2¾ X 5¾
B	◣ ▭	5 ▢	1⅝	2	2⅜	2¾
C	◺	3 ▢	1¼	1½	1¾	2
D	▱	1 ▭	1¾ X 3⅜	2¼ X 4¼	2½ X 5⅜	3 X 6¼
E	▷	1 ▭	1⅛ X 1¼	1⅜ X 1½	1½ X 1¾	1¾ X 2
F	▢ ◺	5 ▢	1⅛	1⅜	1½	1¾
G	▽	1 ▭	2¾ X 3⅛	3⅜ X 4⅛	4⅜ X 4¾	5 X 5¾
H	▭	1 ▭	1⅝ X 4¼	2 X 5½	2⅜ X 6¾	2¾ X 8
I	◣	2 ▣	⅞	1	1⅛	1¼
J	⬠	1 ▱	2½	3¼	3¾	4½
K	◹	1 ▭	1⅞ X 3⅜	2⅜ X 4¼	2¾ X 5⅜	3¼ X 6¼
L	◣	2 ▣	1⅝	2	2⅜	2¾
M	⬡	1 ▭	2¾ X 3⅞	3⅜ X 4¾	4⅜ X 6⅜	5 X 7¼
N	◣	1 ▢	1	1⅛	1⅜	1½
O	⬡	1 ▭	1⅝ X 3⅞	2 X 4⅞	2⅜ X 6 ¼	2¾ X 7¼
P	◣	1 ▭	1 X 2⅝	1⅛ X 3¼	1⅜ X 4	1½ X 4¾
Q	▱	1 ▭	2⅛ X 2⅝	2⅝ X 3¼	3⅛ X 4	3¼ X 4¾
R	▱	2 ▣	1⅝	2	2⅜	2¾
Eye	●	1*	See page 10			

*Fuse on after sewing the complete block.

See page 10

tip

I love Bluebirds! To give the illusion of flight, choose background fabric with swirls or a vertical pattern.

bluebird

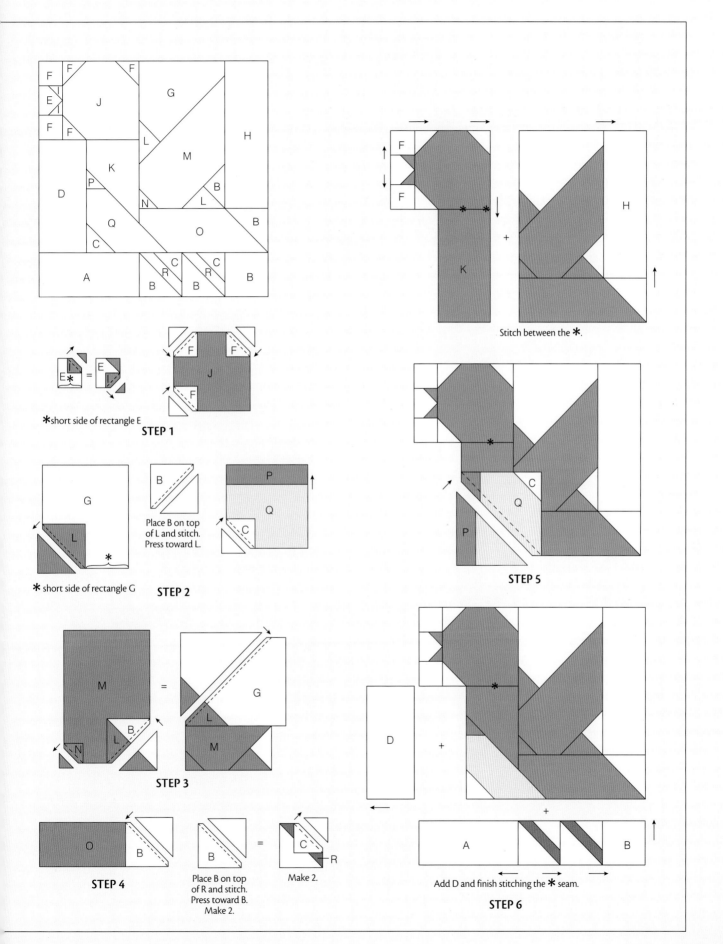

*short side of rectangle E

STEP 1

Place B on top
of L and stitch.
Press toward L.

*short side of rectangle G

STEP 2

STEP 3

STEP 4

Place B on top
of R and stitch.
Press toward B.
Make 2.

Make 2.

Stitch between the *.

STEP 5

Add D and finish stitching the * seam.

STEP 6

basket

(Design by Nancy Johnson-Srebro)

Embellish this basket with hearts and flowers.

USED FOR	SHAPE/ COLOR	NUMBER TO CUT	BLOCK SIZE			
			6"	8"	10"	12"
A	▭	4 ▭	1¼ x 3¼	1½ x 4⅛	1¾ x 5	2 x 6
B	◺	2 □	1½	2	2¼	2½
C	⬠	1 ▭	2¾ x 4	3⅜ x 5	4⅛ x 6¼	5 x 7½
D	▭	2 ▭	⅞ x 1	1 x 1¼	1⅛ x 1½	1¼ x 1½
E	◿	2 □	1¼	1½	1¾	2
F	◢	2 ▪	1¼	1½	1¾	2
G	⬯	1 ▬	1 x 5	1¼ x 6½	1⅜ x 8	1½ x 9½
H	◣◥	2 ▬	1 x 2¾	1¼ x 3⅜	1⅜ x 4⅛	1½ x 5
I	▭	1 ▬	1 x 5¾	1¼ x 7½	1½ x 9¼	1½ x 11
J	⬯	1 ▬	3¼ x 5	4⅛ x 6½	5 x 8	6 x 9½

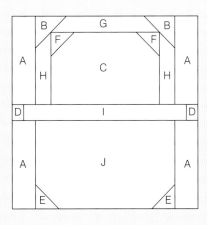

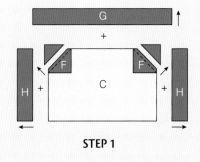

STEP 1

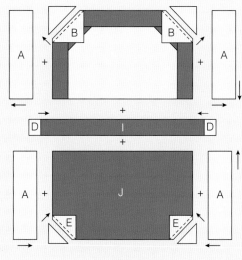

STEP 2

basket

classic jug
(Design by Nancy Johnson-Srebro)

Embellish this jug with stars, birds, hearts; anything!

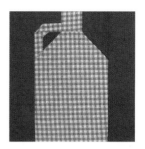

USED FOR	SHAPE/ COLOR	NUMBER TO CUT	BLOCK SIZE			
			6"	8"	10"	12"
A	▭	2 ▭	1¾ x 6½	2 x 8½	2½ x 10½	3 x 12½
B	▭	1 ▭	1½ x 1¾	1¾ x 2⅜	2¼ x 2⅝	2½ x 3
C	◿	1 ▫	⅞	1	1⅛	1¼
D	▭	1 ▭	1⅛ x 1¾	1¼ x 2⅜	1⅝ x 2⅝	1¾ x 3
E	◺	1 ▫	1¾	2⅜	2⅝	3
F	△	1 ▭	1⅜ x 1¾	1⅞ x 2⅜	2 x 2⅝	2¼ x 3
G	⬡	1 ▬	4 x 5½	5½ x 7¼	6½ x 8¾	7½ x 10½
H	▪	1 ▪	1½	1¾	2¼	2½
I	◣	1 ▪	¾	¾	⅞	1
J	◣◢	2 ▬	⅞ x 1¾	1 x 2⅜	1⅛ x 2⅝	1¼ x 3

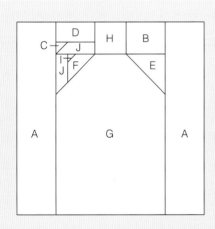

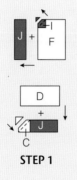

STEP 1

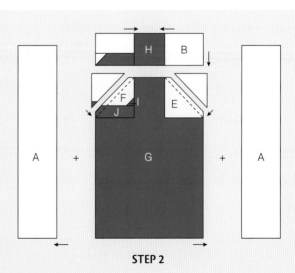

STEP 2

saint nick *(Design by Nancy Johnson-Srebro)*

Dress him up in his best suit and embellish with a beard.

USED FOR	SHAPE/ COLOR	NUMBER TO CUT	BLOCK SIZE			
			6"	9"	12"	15"
A		2	2¼ x 2½	3⅛ x 3½	4 x 4½	4⅞ x 5½
B		2	1¾ x 4½	2⅜ x 6½	3 x 8½	3⅝ x 10½
C		2	1¼ x 1½	1⅝ x 2	2 x 2½	2⅜ x 3
D		2	⅞ x 1½	1 x 2	1¼ x 2½	1⅜ x 3
E		5	1	1¼	1½	1¾
F		2	1 x 2½	1¼ x 3½	1½ x 4½	1¾ x 5½
G		2	1¾ x 3	2⅜ x 4¼	3 x 5½	3⅝ x 6¾
H		2	1 x 2¼	1¼ x 3⅛	1½ x 4	1¾ x 4⅞
I		1	1¼ x 2½	1⅝ x 3½	2 x 4½	2⅜ x 5½
J		2	1	1¼	1½	1¾
K		1	¾ x 3	⅞ x 4¼	1 x 5½	1⅛ x 6¾
L		2	¾ x 1	⅞ x 1¼	1 x 1½	1⅛ x 1¾
M		2	1½ x 1¾	2 x 2⅜	2½ x 3	3 x 3⅝
N		2	1 x 1½	1¼ x 2	1½ x 2½	1¾ x 3
O		1	1½	2	2½	3
P		2	⅞ x 1½	1⅛ x 2	1¼ x 2½	1½ x 3
Eyes, Beard, Mittens and Buttons ◦ ⌣ ◖ ◦		2*, 1*, 2*, 3*	See page 10			

*Fuse on after sewing the complete block.

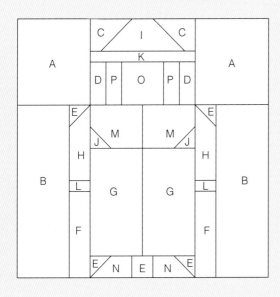

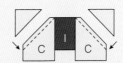

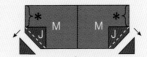

*short side of rectangle M

STEP 1

tip

Embellish this old-timer
with a bag of toys or
candy canes to brighten
any holiday décor.

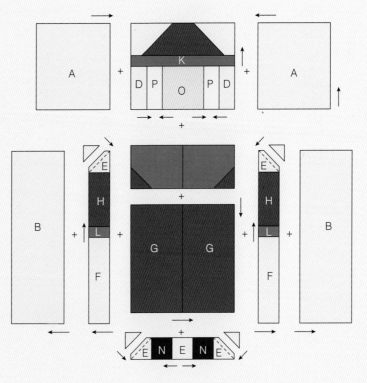

STEP 2

apple

(Design by Jennifer Srebro)

Apples come in many different colors: red, green, or yellow.

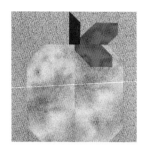 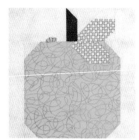 

USED FOR	SHAPE/ COLOR	NUMBER TO CUT	BLOCK SIZE			
			6"	8"	10"	12"
A	▭	1 ▭	2 x 3¼	2½ x 4⅛	3 x 5	3½ x 6
B	◺	1 ☐	1¾	2⅛	2⅝	3
C	◺	2 ☐	1	1⅛	1⅜	1½
D	▭	1 ▭	1½ x 2	1⅞ x 2½	2⅛ x 3	2½ x 3½
E	◺	4 ☐	1¼	1½	1¾	2
F	▱	1 ▭	1 x 2¼	1⅛ x 2⅞	1⅜ x 3½	1½ x 4
G	▭	2 ▭	1¼ x 5	1½ x 6½	1¾ x 8	2 x 9½
H	◣	1 ■	1 x 2	1⅛ x 2½	1⅜ x 3	1½ x 3½
I	⬠	2 ▬	1½ x 2¼	1⅞ x 2⅞	2⅛ x 3½	2½ x 4
J	◣	1 ■	1¼	1½	1¾	2
K	◢	1 ▬	1 x 1½	1⅛ x 1⅞	1¼ x 2⅛	1½ x 2½
L	◿	1 ■	1	1⅛	1⅜	1½
M	⬡	1 ▬	2¾ x 5	3½ x 6½	4¼ x 8	5 x 9½
N	⬡	1 ▬	2¾ x 4	3½ x 5⅛	4¼ x 6⅜	5 x 7½

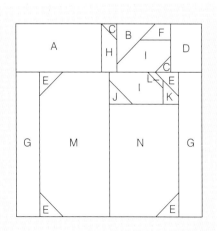

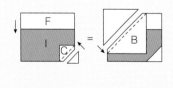

STEP 1

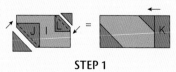

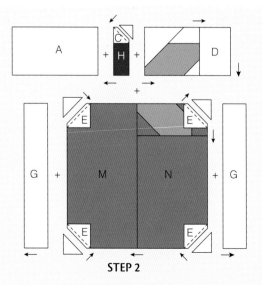

STEP 2

apple

coffee mug

(Design by Janet McCarroll)

If you have hot chocolate in this mug, don't forget to embellish with marshmallows!

USED FOR	SHAPE/ COLOR	NUMBER TO CUT	BLOCK SIZE			
			6"	8"	10"	12"
A		1	1¾ x 6½	2⅛ x 8½	2½ x 10½	3 x 12½
B		2	1 x 5¼	1⅛ x 6⅞	1¼ x 8½	1½ x 10
C		1	1 x 1¾	1⅛ x 2¼	1⅜ x 2⅝	1½ x 3
D		3	1	1⅛	1⅜	1½
E		1	1¼ x 2¾	1⅝ x 3¾	1¾ x 4¼	2 x 5
F		1	1¼	1⅝	1¾	2
G		1	1 x 1¼	1⅛ x 1⅝	1⅜ x 1¾	1½ x 2
H		1	1¼ x 1¾	1½ x 2¼	1¾ x 2⅝	2 x 3
I		1	4¼ x 5¼	5½ x 6⅞	6⅞ x 8½	8 x 10
J		1	1 x 1¾	1⅛ x 2¼	1⅜ x 2⅝	1½ x 3
K		1	1 x 3	1⅛ x 4	1⅜ x 4⅝	1½ x 5½
L		1	¾	¾	⅞	1
M		1	1¼ x 1½	1⅝ x 1⅞	1¾ x 2⅛	2 x 2½
N		1	1	1⅛	1⅜	1½

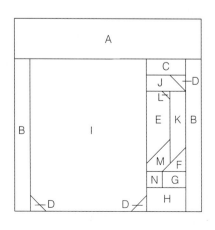

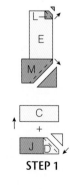

STEP 1

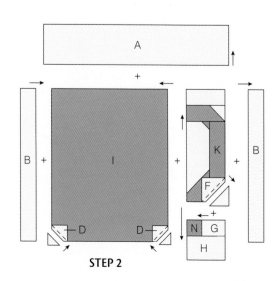

STEP 2

cardinal

(Design by Nancy Johnson-Srebro)

Simply change the color to brown to make a female cardinal.

USED FOR	SHAPE/ COLOR	NUMBER TO CUT	BLOCK SIZE			
			6"	8"	10"	12"
A	▭	1 ▭	1¾ X 4	2 X 5⅛	2½ X 6⅜	3 X 7½
B	▭	2 ▭	1½ X 1⅝	1⅞ X 2	2⅛ X 2⅜	2½ X 2¾
C	▭	1 ▭	1¼ X 1½	1⅝ X 1⅞	1¾ X 2⅛	2 X 2½
D	▭	1 ▭	1 X 1¾	1¼ X 2⅛	1¼ X 2¾	1½ X 3
E	◺	1 ▢	2⅛	2⅝	3¼	3¾
F	◺	3 ▢	1	1⅛	1⅜	1½
G	◺	1 ▭	1⅞ X 2⅛	2¼ X 2⅝	2⅞ X 3¼	3¼ X 3¾
H	◺	1 ▢	1⅜	1⅝	2	2¼
I	◺	1 ▢	⅞	1	1¼	1¼
J	▭	1 ▭	3 X 4	3⅞ X 5¼	4⅝ X 6⅜	5½ X 7½
K	▭	1 ▭	⅞ X 1⅜	1 X 1¾	1¼ X 1⅞	1¼ X 2¼
L	◹	1 ▭	1⅜ X 2⅝	1¾ X 3¼	1⅞ X 3⅞	2¼ X 4¾
M	▭	1 ▭	1¼ X 2⅛	1⅜ X 2⅝	1⅝ X 3¼	2 X 3¾
N	◣	1 ▪	1⅜	1¾	1⅞	2¼
O	◣	3 ▪	1	1⅛	1⅜	1½
P	⬟	1 ▬	2⅛ X 2¼	2⅝ X 2⅞	3¼ X 3½	3¾ X 4
Q	▱	1 ▬	1¼ X 1⅞	1⅝ X 2¼	1¾ X 2⅞	2 X 3¼
R	⬢	1 ▬	1⅞ X 4¼	2¼ X 5½	2⅞ X 6⅞	3¼ X 8
S	▱	1 ▬	1⅝ X 5¼	2 X 7	2⅜ X 8½	2¾ X 10
T	▱	1 ▪	1 X 1¾	1⅛ X 2⅛	1⅜ X 2¾	1½ X 3
U	▭	2 ▭	¾ X 1½	⅞ X 1⅞	⅞ X 2⅛	1 X 2½
Eye and Beak ● ▷		1*, 1*	See page 10			

*Fuse on after sewing the complete block.

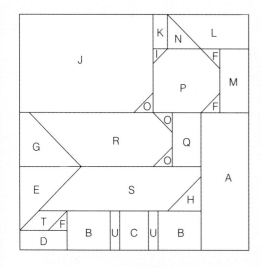

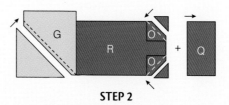

STEP 2

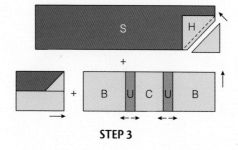

STEP 3

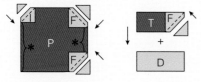

*short side of rectangle P

STEP 1

t¡p

For a primitive look, use small red-and-black check fabric. A green background will hide your cardinal in an evergreen.

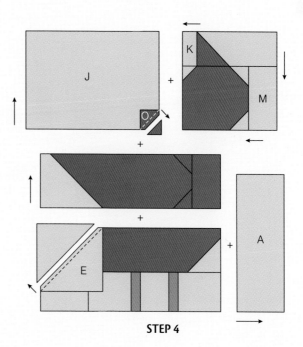

STEP 4

fancy petunias

(Design by Nancy Johnson-Srebro)

A row of multi-colored flowers makes a stunning border for a quilt.

USED FOR	SHAPE/ COLOR	NUMBER TO CUT	BLOCK SIZE			
			6"	8"	10"	12"
A	▭	1 ▭	$1\frac{5}{8} \times 3\frac{1}{2}$	$2 \times 4\frac{1}{2}$	$2\frac{3}{8} \times 5\frac{1}{2}$	$2\frac{3}{4} \times 6\frac{1}{2}$
B	◺	8 ▢	$1\frac{1}{2}$	$1\frac{3}{4}$	$2\frac{1}{8}$	$2\frac{1}{2}$
C	◺	6 ▢	$1\frac{3}{4}$	$2\frac{1}{8}$	$2\frac{5}{8}$	3
D	▱▱	2 ▭	$1\frac{3}{4} \times 2\frac{7}{8}$	$2\frac{1}{8} \times 3\frac{5}{8}$	$2\frac{5}{8} \times 4\frac{1}{2}$	$3 \times 5\frac{1}{4}$
E	▱▱	4 ▭	$\frac{7}{8} \times 2\frac{3}{8}$	1×3	$1\frac{1}{8} \times 3\frac{5}{8}$	$1\frac{1}{4} \times 4\frac{1}{4}$
F	▱▱	4 ▰	$1\frac{3}{8} \times 2\frac{3}{8}$	$1\frac{5}{8} \times 3$	$2 \times 3\frac{5}{8}$	$2\frac{1}{4} \times 4\frac{1}{4}$
G	▬	1 ▰	$1 \times 3\frac{1}{2}$	$1\frac{1}{4} \times 4\frac{1}{2}$	$1\frac{1}{4} \times 5\frac{1}{2}$	$1\frac{1}{2} \times 6\frac{1}{2}$
H	▬	1 ▰	$1 \times 2\frac{3}{8}$	$1\frac{1}{4} \times 3$	$1\frac{1}{4} \times 3\frac{5}{8}$	$1\frac{1}{2} \times 4\frac{1}{4}$
I	◺	4* ▪	1	$1\frac{1}{8}$	$1\frac{3}{8}$	$1\frac{1}{2}$
J	◢	4* ▪	2	$2\frac{1}{2}$	3	$3\frac{1}{2}$
K	◢	4* ▫	2	$2\frac{1}{2}$	3	$3\frac{1}{2}$

*Using different colors, repeat for the second flower.

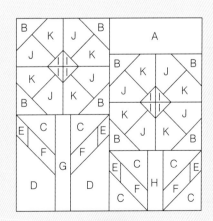

Place J on top of K and
stitch. Press toward J. Make
4 sets for each flower.

STEP 1

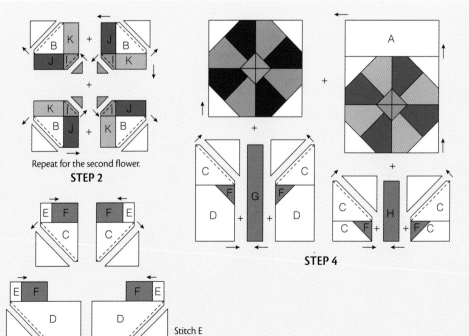

Repeat for the second flower.
STEP 2

Stitch E
to F first.

STEP 3

STEP 4

fancy petunias

mr. frosty

(Design by Nancy Johnson-Srebro)

Watch the fun begin when you embellish this gentleman with different shapes for eyes, nose, and mouth.

USED FOR	SHAPE/ COLOR	NUMBER TO CUT	BLOCK SIZE			
			6"	8"	10"	12"
A	⬠	1 ▭	2¾ x 5	3½ x 6½	4¼ x 8	5 x 9½
B	⬓	1 ▭	2½ x 3	3¼ x 3¾	3⅞ x 4¾	4½ x 5½
C	▬	1 ▬	1 x 4	1¼ x 5¼	1⅜ x 6½	1½ x 7½
D	▬	1 ▬	1¾ x 2½	2 x 3¼	2½ x 3¾	3 x 4½
E	▬	2 ▬	1¾ x 2½	2 x 3⅛	2½ x 3⅞	3 x 4½
F	▬	2 ▬	1 x 2½	1¼ x 3¼	1⅜ x 3⅞	1½ x 4½
G	▬	2 ▬	1¾ x 3	2⅛ x 4	2½ x 4¾	3 x 5½
H	◺	2 ▪	2	2½	3	3½
I	◿	2 ▪	1	1⅛	1⅜	1½
J	▬	2 ▬	1¼ x 2¾	1½ x 3½	1¾ x 4¼	2 x 5
Eyes, nose, and mouth	● ◣ ●	2*, 1*, 3*	2*, 1*, 3*	See page 10		

*Fuse on after sewing the complete block.

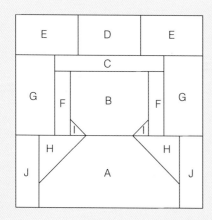

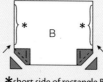

*short side of rectangle B
STEP 1

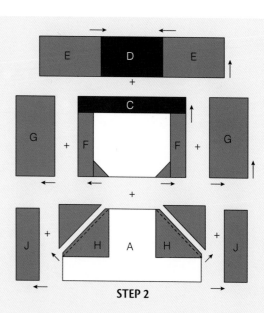

STEP 2

doll buggy

(Design by Arlene Begey Shea)

Let your daughter or granddaughter help you choose the fabrics for this buggy.

  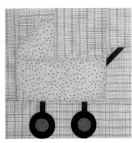

USED FOR	SHAPE/ COLOR	NUMBER TO CUT	BLOCK SIZE			
			6"	8"	10"	12"
A	▭	1 ▭	2⅛ X 2¼	2⅝ X 2⅞	3¼ X 3½	3¾ X 4
B	▢	1 ▢	2¼	2⅞	3½	4
C	▭	1 ▭	2¼ X 2⅝	2⅞ X 3¼	3½ X 4	4 X 4¾
D	▱	1 ▭	1¾ X 3	2 X 3⅞	2½ X 4⅝	3 X 5½
E	◺	2 ▢	1	1⅛	1⅜	1½
F	◺	1 ▢	1¼	1½	1¾	2
G	▭	1 ▭	1 X 4¾	1⅛ X 6⅛	1⅜ X 7½	1½ X 9
H	◸	1 ▢	1¾	2	2½	3
I	▭	1 ▭	1 X 2¼	1⅛ X 2¾	1¼ X 3½	1½ X 4
J	▭	1 ▭	2¾ X 3	3⅜ X 4⅛	4¼ X 4⅝	5 X 5½
K	▭	1 ▭	1¾ X 2¼	2 X 2¾	2½ X 3⅜	3 X 4
L	◢	1 ◼	2¼	2¾	3½	4
M	▬	1 ▬	2½ X 4¾	3¼ X 6⅜	3¾ X 7⅝	4½ X 9
N	◣	1 ◼	1⅜	1⅝	2	2¼
O	▬	2 ▬	¾ X 2¼	⅞ X 2⅞	⅞ X 3½	1 X 4
Wheels and hubcaps ●○		2*, 2*	See page 10			

*Fuse on after sewing the complete block.

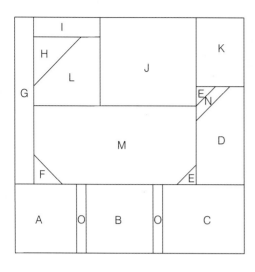

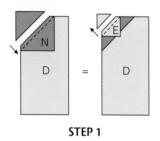

STEP 1

tip

Be sure you leave a ¼" seam allowance at the bottom of the block when you fuse or appliqué the wheels on. Otherwise, your buggy will have "flat tires" when you add lattice strips!

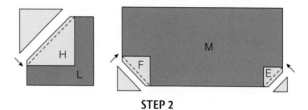

STEP 2

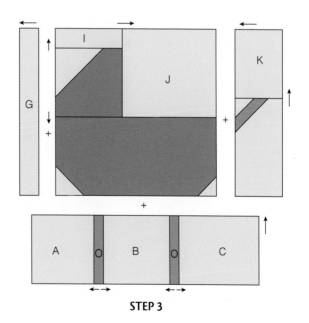

STEP 3

gabby the goose
(Design by Nancy Johnson-Srebro)

You could easily embellish this goose with bows, hearts, or even a wreath around its neck.

USED FOR	SHAPE/ COLOR	NUMBER TO CUT	BLOCK SIZE			
			6"	8"	10"	12"
A	▭	1 ▭	1¼ x 3	1½ x 4	1¾ x 4½	2 x 5½
B	◺	3 ▢	⅞	1	1⅛	1¼
C	◹	1 ▭	1⅝ x 4	2 x 5	2⅜ x 6½	2¾ x 7½
D	▢	1 ▭	4 x 4⅜	5 x 5⅝	6½ x 7	7½ x 8¼
E	◺	1 ▢	2	2½	3	3½
F	▱	1 ▭	3 x 5¾	4 x 7½	4½ x 9¼	5½ x 11
G	◥	1 ▪	1½	1⅞	2	2½
H	◣	1 ▪	⅞	1	1⅛	1¼
I	▱	1 ▭	1½ x 4	1⅞ x 5	2⅛ x 6½	2½ x 7½
J	◹	1 ▭	1⅛ x 1⅝	1⅜ x 2	1½ x 2⅜	1¾ x 2¾
K	◣	1 ▪	1 x 1⅝	1⅛ x 2	1⅜ x 2⅜	1½ x 2¾
Eye	●	1*	See page 10			

*Fuse on after sewing the complete block.

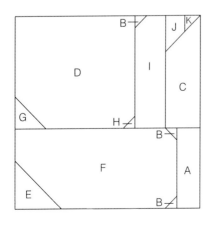

STEP 1

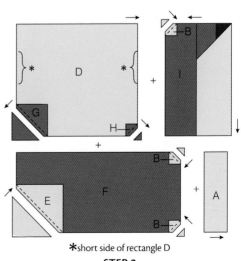

*short side of rectangle D

STEP 2

bernie the bumblebee
(Design by Nancy Johnson-Srebro)

You know it's summer when you see this guy flying around.

  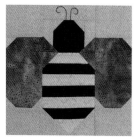

USED FOR	SHAPE/ COLOR	NUMBER TO CUT	BLOCK SIZE			
			6"	8"	10"	12"
A	▭	2 ▭	2 x 2¼	2¾ x 2⅞	2⅞ x 3½	3½ x 4
B	▭	1 ▭	1¼ x 3	1¾ x 3¾	1⅝ x 4½	2 x 5½
C	◹	8 ▫	1	1⅛	1⅜	1½
D	◸▱	2 ▭	1 x 2	1⅛ x 2½	1¼ x 3	1½ x 3½
E	▭	2 ▭	1¾ x 2¼	2⅛ x 2⅞	2½ x 3½	3 x 4
F	◺	2 ▫	1¾	2⅛	2½	3
G	▱	2 ▭	2¼ x 3¾	2⅞ x 4⅝	3½ x 6⅛	4 x 7
H	◺	4 ▫	1¼	1½	1¾	2
I	⬡	1 ◼	2	2½	3	3½
J	◣▼▬	3 ◼	1 x 3	1⅛ x 3¾	1⅜ x 4½	1½ x 5½
K	◺▭	3 ▭	1 x 3	1⅛ x 3¾	1⅜ x 4½	1½ x 5½
L	▽	1 ▭	1¼ x 3	1½ x 3¾	1⅝ x 4½	2 x 5½

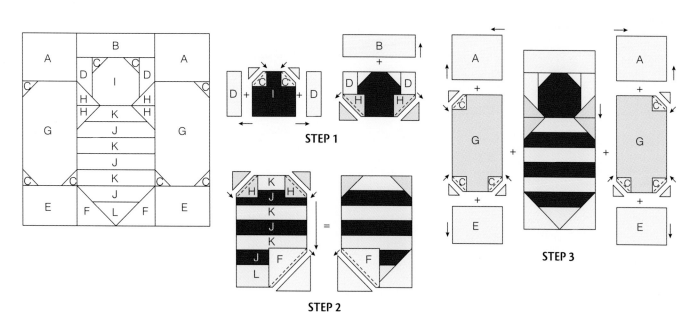

STEP 1

STEP 2

STEP 3

high flyer

(Design by Nancy Johnson-Srebro)

Try using a dark background with light-colored mountains.

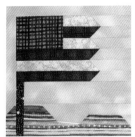  

USED FOR	SHAPE/ COLOR	NUMBER TO CUT	BLOCK SIZE			
			6"	9"	12"	15"
A		1	1 x 5½	1¼ x 8	1½ x 10½	1¾ x 13
B		1	1 x 6	1¼ x 8¾	1½ x 11½	1¾ x 14¼
C		7	1 x 2½	1¼ x 3½	1½ x 4½	1¾ x 5½
D		1	1½ x 5⅝	2 x 8¼	2½ x 10¾	3 x 13¼
E		1	1½ x 2¾	2 x 4	2½ x 5	3 x 6
F		1	1	1¼	1½	1¾
G		1	2 x 2¾	2¾ x 3⅞	3½ x 5	4¼ x 6⅛
H		2	1 x 2¼	1¼ x 3⅛	1½ x 4	1¾ x 4⅞
I		1	1 x 4½	1¼ x 6½	1½ x 8½	1¾ x 10½
J		1	1 x 2¼	1¼ x 3⅛	1½ x 4	1¾ x 4⅞
K		2	1 x 4½	1¼ x 6½	1½ x 8½	1¾ x 10½
L		1	⅞ x 3	1 x 4¼	1¼ x 5½	1½ x 6¾
M		1	1 x 2	1¼ x 2¾	1½ x 3½	1¾ x 4¼
N		1	2 x 2⅞	2¾ x 4	3½ x 5¼	4¼ x 6½
O		1	1 x 2¾	1¼ x 4	1½ x 5	1¾ x 6
P		1	1	1¼	1½	1¾
Q		1	1½ x 2½	2 x 3½	2½ x 4½	3 x 5½

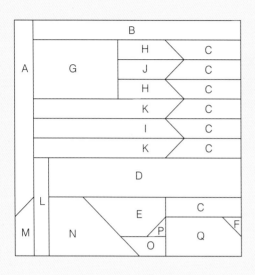

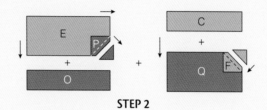

STEP 2

Make 2.

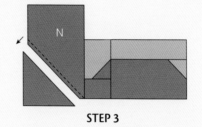

STEP 3

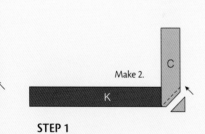

Make 2.

STEP 1

tip

Use different fabrics for the hills to simulate the seasons. Add a star to the flag to create your unique interpretation.

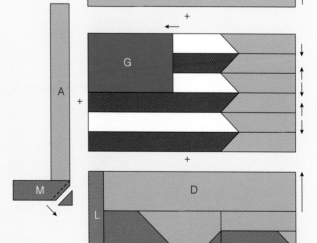

STEP 4

heart to heart
(Design by Nancy Johnson-Srebro)

Have fun switching the placement of the light and dark colors in the large and small hearts.

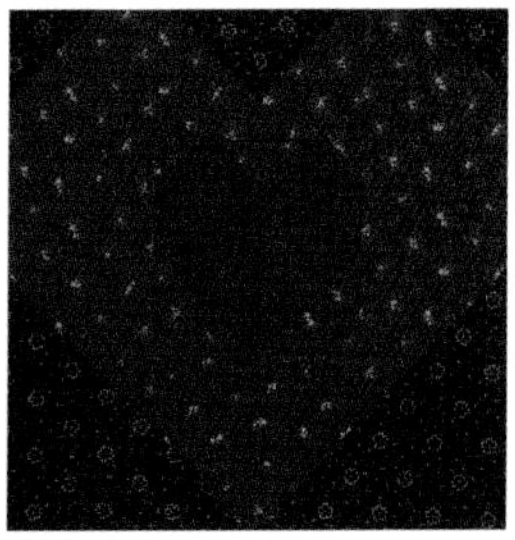

USED FOR	SHAPE/ COLOR	NUMBER TO CUT	BLOCK SIZE			
			6"	8"	10"	12"
A	◺	4 ▨	1½	1¾	2¼	2½
B	◹	2 ▨	3½	4½	5½	6½
C	◣	4 ■	1	1	1¼	1½
D	◣	2 ■	1¾	2⅛	2½	3
E	▱	2 ▭	2¼ x 6½	2⅞ x 8½	3½ x 10½	4 x 12½
F	◣	2 ▭	1¾ x 2	2⅛ x 2½	2½ x 3	3 x 3½
G	▽	1 ▭	2½ x 3	3¼ x 3¾	4 x 4½	4½ x 5½
H	⬠	2 ▭	1¾ x 3	2⅛ x 3¾	2½ x 4½	3 x 5½

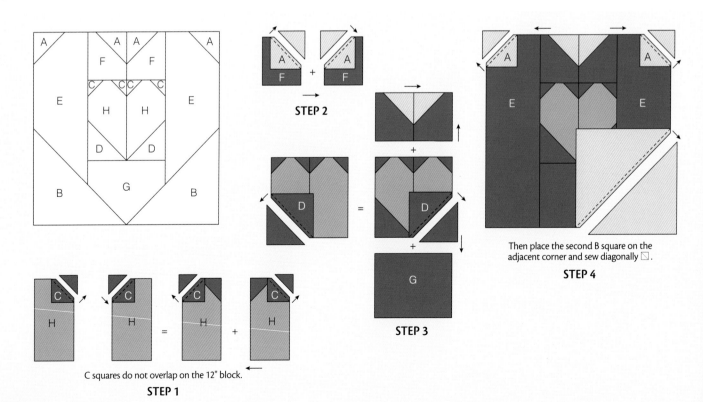

STEP 2

STEP 3

Then place the second B square on the adjacent corner and sew diagonally ◺.

STEP 4

C squares do not overlap on the 12" block.

STEP 1

heart to heart

happy birthday cake!

(Design by Frank Srebro)

Have fun decorating this cake.

USED FOR	SHAPE/ COLOR	NUMBER TO CUT	BLOCK SIZE			
			6"	8"	10"	12"
A	☐	2 ☐	3	3⅞	4⅝	5½
B	▭	2 ▭	1¼ x 3½	1⅜ x 4½	1½ x 5½	1¾ x 6½
C	◿	6 ☐	1	1⅛	1⅜	1½
D	▽	1 ▬	1 x 6½	1⅛ x 8½	1⅜ x 10½	1½ x 12½
E	▱	2 ▱	1¾ x 5	2⅛ x 6¾	2½ x 8½	3 x 10
F	▭	1 ▬	1 x 5	1¼ x 6¾	1½ x 8½	1½ x 10
G	▭	1 ▬	1½ x 2	1¾ x 2⅝	2¼ x 2⅞	2½ x 3½
H	◼	1 ◼	1½	1¾	2¼	2½

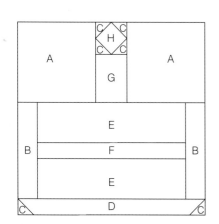

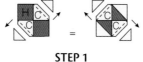

STEP 1

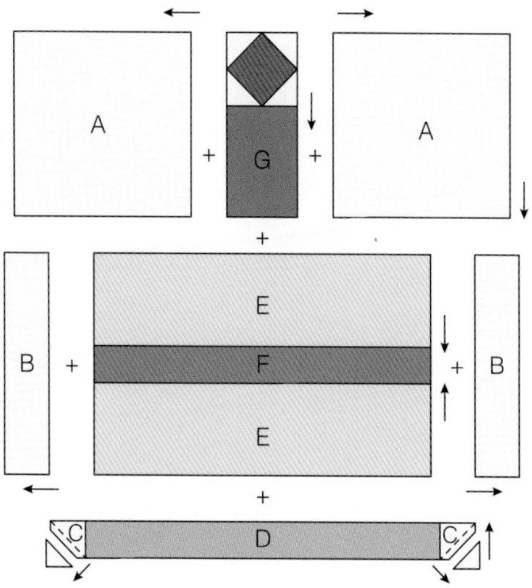

STEP 2

sea turtle *(Design by Liz Aneloski)*

Make a family of sea turtles and watch them swim away!

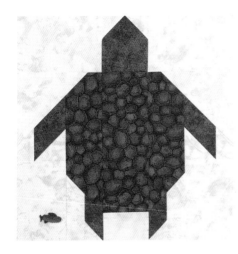

USED FOR	SHAPE/ COLOR	NUMBER TO CUT	BLOCK SIZE			
			6"	8"	10"	12"
A	▭	2 ▭	2 x 2⅞	2½ x 3⅝	3 x 4½	3½ x 5¼
B	◺	2 ▢	1⅛	1⅜	1½	1¾
C	◺	2 ▢	2½	3⅛	3⅞	4½
D	▱◿	2 ▭	1 x 2⅞	1¼ x 3⅝	1⅜ x 4½	1½ x 5¼
E	◺	2 ▢	1⅜	1⅝	1⅞	2¼
F	◹◿	2 ▭	1 x 2¼	1⅛ x 2¾	1⅜ x 3½	1½ x 4
G	▭	2 ▭	1⅞ x 2⅝	2⅜ x 3⅜	2¾ x 4	3¼ x 4¾
H	▭	1 ▭	1¼ x 1¾	1½ x 2¼	1¾ x 2½	2 x 3
I	◺	2 ▢	1	1⅛	1⅜	1½
J	◣◢	2 ▮	1 x 2¼	1⅛ x 2¾	1⅜ x 3½	1½ x 4
K	◣◢	2 ▮	1⅜ x 2⅞	1⅝ x 3⅝	1⅞ x 4½	2¼ x 5¼
L	▮	1 ▮	1¾ x 2	2¼ x 2½	2½ x 3	3 x 3½
M	▬	1 ▮	1¾ x 4¼	2¼ x 5½	2½ x 6¾	3 x 8
N	▰	2 ▮	1½ x 4¼	1¾ x 5½	2¼ x 6¾	2½ x 8

tip

For a dramatic look, use large printed fabric for the background and solid colors for the turtle.

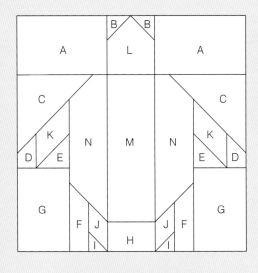

*short side of rectangle L

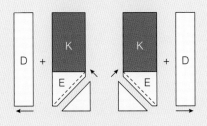

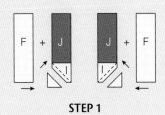

STEP 1

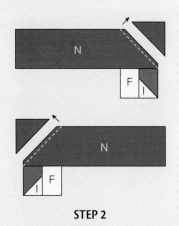

STEP 2

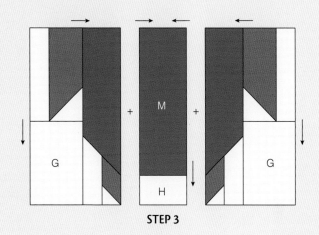

STEP 3

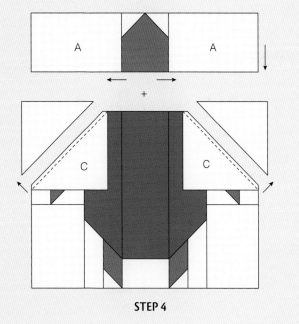

STEP 4

whirlybird
(Design by Nancy Johnson-Srebro)

What child wouldn't love to help pick fabric for this block?

USED FOR	SHAPE/ COLOR	NUMBER TO CUT	BLOCK SIZE			
			6"	8"	10"	12"
A		1	1⅛ x 6½	1⅜ x 8½	1⅝ x 10½	1¾ x 12½
B		1	1½ x 2	1¾ x 2½	2⅛ x 3	2½ x 3½
C		2	1⅛ x 1¼	1¼ x 1½	1½ x 1⅞	1¾ x 2
D		1	1⅛ x 2	1¼ x 2½	1½ x 2⅞	1¾ x 3½
E		1	1½ x 4	1¾ x 5⅛	2⅛ x 6¼	2½ x 7½
F		4	1	1⅛	1⅜	1½
G		1	2	2½	3	3½
H		1	1½ x 2¼	1⅞ x 2⅞	2⅛ x 3⅜	2½ x 4
I		1	1½	1⅞	2⅛	2½
J		1	1¼ x 3¾	1½ x 4⅞	1¾ x 5⅞	2 x 7
K		1	1¼ x 2⅞	1½ x 3⅝	1¾ x 4½	2 x 5¼
L		1	1⅛	1⅜	1½	1¾
M		1	1⅛ x 2	1⅜ x 2⅝	1½ x 2⅞	1¾ x 3½
N		1	1 x 4⅛	1⅛ x 5⅜	1⅜ x 6½	1½ x 7¾
O		1	1 x 2⅞	1⅛ x 3⅝	1⅜ x 4½	1½ x 5¼
P		1	⅞	1	1⅛	1¼
Q		1	⅞ x 1⅞	1 x 2⅜	1⅛ x 2¾	1¼ x 3¼
R		2	1⅛ x 2⅞	1⅜ x 3⅝	1½ x 4½	1¾ x 5¼
S		1	3	3⅞	4⅝	5½
T		1	1⅛	1⅜	1½	1¾
U		1	2 x 2¼	2½ x 2⅞	3 x 3⅜	3½ x 4
V		1	1¼ x 1½	1½ x 1⅞	1⅞ x 2⅛	2 x 2½
W		1	⅞ x 4	1 x 5¼	1⅛ x 6⅜	1¼ x 7½
X		2	¾ x 1⅛	⅞ x 1¼	⅞ x 1½	1 x 1¾
Y		2	⅞	1	1⅛	1¼
Z		1	1¼ x 2	1½ x 2½	1⅞ x 3	2 x 3½

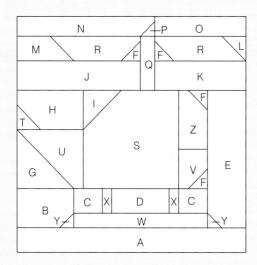

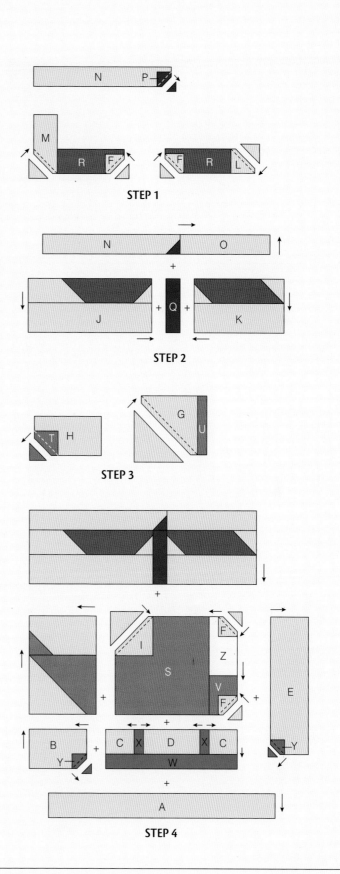

tip The blades will appear to be moving if you use striped fabric. Try olive green for a military helicopter or use white for a TV newscopter.

STEP 1

STEP 2

STEP 3

STEP 4

kuffles the cat

(Design by Nancy Johnson-Srebro)

Embellish with buttons for the eyes and a small pompom for the nose.

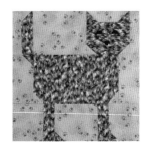

USED FOR	SHAPE/ COLOR	NUMBER TO CUT	BLOCK SIZE			
			6"	9"	12"	15"
A		1	2½ x 3	3½ x 4¼	4½ x 5½	5½ x 6¾
B		3	1 x 2½	1¼ x 3½	1½ x 4½	1¾ x 5½
C		5	1	1¼	1½	1¾
D		2	1½ x 2¾	2 x 3⅞	2½ x 5	3 x 6⅛
E		2	2 x 2¼	2¾ x 3⅛	3½ x 4	4¼ x 4⅞
F		1	2¼ x 2½	3⅛ x 3½	4 x 4½	4⅞ x 5½
G		2	1 x 2¼	1¼ x 3⅛	1½ x 4	1¾ x 4⅞
H		1	2¾ x 4½	3⅞ x 6½	5 x 8½	6⅛ x 10½
I		5	1	1¼	1½	1¾
J		1	1 x 2½	1¼ x 3½	1½ x 4½	1¾ x 5½
K		1	2 x 2½	2¾ x 3½	3½ x 4½	4¼ x 5½
Eyes and nose		2*, 1*	See page 10			

*Fuse on after sewing the complete block.

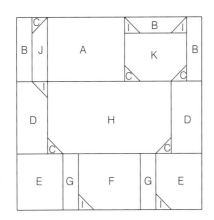

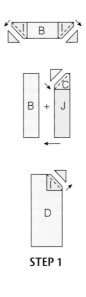

STEP 1

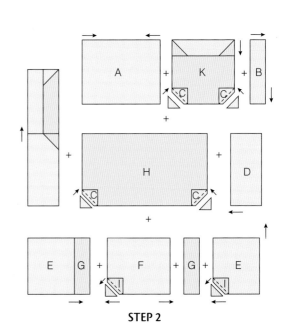

STEP 2

hurricane lamp

(Design by Nancy Johnson-Srebro)

Have fun choosing fabrics for an antique look.

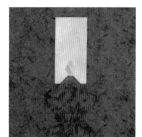

USED FOR	SHAPE/ COLOR		NUMBER TO CUT		BLOCK SIZE			
					6"	8"	10"	12"
A			2		2¼ x 6½	2⅞ x 8½	3⅜ x 10½	4 x 12½
B			2		1 x 4	1⅛ x 5⅛	1⅜ x 6⅜	1½ x 7½
C			1		1 x 2	1⅛ x 2½	1⅜ x 3	1½ x 3½
D			6		1	1⅛	1⅜	1½
E			2		⅞ x 1	1 x 1⅛	1⅛ x 1⅜	1¼ x 1½
F			1		2 x 3½	2½ x 4½	3 x 5½	3½ x 6½
G			1		1⅞ x 3	2⅜ x 3¾	2¾ x 4¾	3¼ x 5½
H			1		⅞ x 2	1 x 2½	1⅛ x 3	1¼ x 3½
I			1		1¼ x 3	1½ x 3¾	1¾ x 4¾	2 x 5½
Wick			1**		⅝ x 1½	¾ x 1¾	⅞ x 2	1 x 2½
Flame			1*		See page 10			

*Fuse on after sewing the complete block.

**Cut angles at 45-degrees. 45° 45° Fuse to F before sewing the complete block.

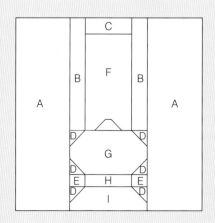
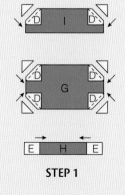
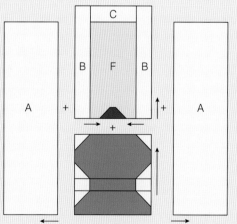

STEP 1

Fuse the wick to F before stitching to the G unit.

STEP 2

tug boat *(Design by Nancy Johnson-Srebro)*

Let your child help you choose the fabrics for this boat.

 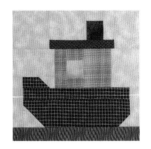 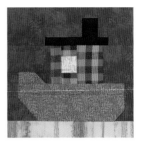

USED FOR	SHAPE/ COLOR	NUMBER TO CUT	BLOCK SIZE			
			6"	8"	10"	12"
A	☐	1 ☐	2¼	2⅞	3½	4
B	▭	1 ▭	1⅞ X 2¼	2⅜ X 2⅞	2⅞ X 3⅛	3¼ X 4
C	▭ ◿	2 ▭	1 X 1¼	1⅛ X 1½	1⅜ X 1⅞	1½ X 2
D	▭	1 ▭	1 X 1⅞	1⅛ X 2⅜	1⅜ X 2⅞	1½ X 3¼
E	▭	1 ▭	1¾ X 2¼	2⅛ X 2⅞	2⅝ X 3½	3 X 4
F	▭	1 ▭	2 X 2¼	2⅜ X 2⅞	3 X 3⅜	3½ X 4
G	▭	1 ▭	1¾ X 2½	2¼ X 3⅛	2½ X 3⅞	3 X 4½
H	☐ ◺	2 ☐	1	1⅛	1⅜	1½
I	▭	2 ▭	1 X 2¼	1⅛ X 2¾	1⅜ X 3⅜	1½ X 4
J	◿	1 ☐	1½	1¾	2⅛	2½
K	▬	1 ▬	1¼ X 6½	1½ X 8½	1¾ X 10½	2 X 12½
L	▬	1 ▬	1¾ X 5½	2⅛ X 7¼	2½ X 8¾	3 X 10½
M	▬	1 ▬	1 X 5½	1⅛ X 7¼	1⅜ X 8¾	1½ X 10½
N	▬	1 ▬	1 X 1¾	1⅛ X 2⅛	1⅜ X 2½	1½ X 3
O	▬	1 ▬	1 X 2¼	1⅛ X 2⅞	1⅜ X 3⅜	1½ X 4
P	▬	2 ▬	1 X 1¼	1⅛ X 1⅝	1⅜ X 1⅝	1½ X 2
Q	▬	1 ▬	1¾ X 2¼	2¼ X 2⅞	2⅝ X 3⅜	3 X 4
R	☐	1 ☐	1¼	1⅝	1⅝	2
S	▬	1 ▬	1¼ X 1⅜	1½ X 1¾	1⅞ X 2	2 X 2¼
T	▬	1 ▬	⅞ X 3½	1 X 4½	1⅛ X 5⅜	1¼ X 6½

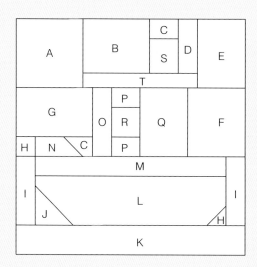

tip

Use fabric that looks like moving water. Add some smoke from the stack and watch this boat chug along.

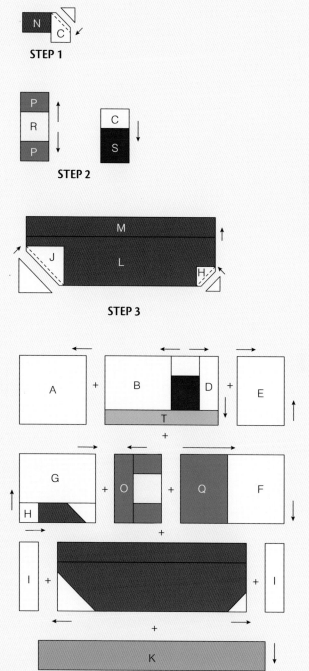

STEP 1

STEP 2

STEP 3

STEP 4

farm house

(Design by Nancy Johnson-Srebro)

If only houses could talk! Farm houses would have many a story to tell.

USED FOR	SHAPE/ COLOR	NUMBER TO CUT	BLOCK SIZE			
			6"	9"	12"	15"
A		1	2 x 4	2¾ x 5¾	3½ x 7½	4¼ x 9¼
B		1	1¾ x 4	2⅜ x 5¾	3 x 7½	3⅝ x 9¼
C		1	3	4¼	5½	6¾
D		1	1½ x 6½	2⅛ x 9½	2½ x 12½	2⅞ x 15½
E		1	1¼ x 3⅝	1½ x 5¼	2 x 6¾	2½ x 8¼
F		1	1¼ x 2⅝	1½ x 3¾	2 x 4¾	2½ x 5¾
G		1	2½ x 6½	3½ x 9½	4½ x 12½	5½ x 15½
H		2	1½ x 2¾	2 x 3⅞	2½ x 5	3 x 6⅛
I		2	1¼ x 2¾	1⅝ x 3⅞	2 x 5	2⅜ x 6⅛
J		1	1¼ x 2	1⅝ x 2¾	2 x 3½	2⅜ x 4¼
K		2	1¼ x 2	1⅝ x 2¾	2 x 3½	2⅜ x 4¼
L		1	1¼	1½	2	2½
M		1	1½ x 2¾	2 x 3⅞	2½ x 5	3 x 6⅛
N		1	1¼ x 4	1⅝ x 5¾	2 x 7½	2⅜ x 9¼

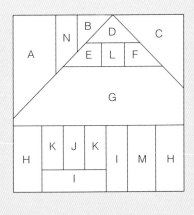

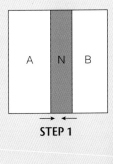

STEP 1

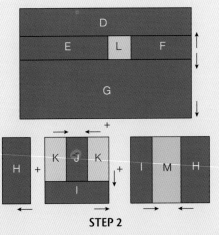

STEP 2

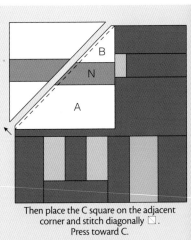

Then place the C square on the adjacent corner and stitch diagonally ◻. Press toward C.

STEP 3

52 farm house

little red wagon

(Design by Nancy Johnson-Srebro)

Fill this wagon with toys and see your children's eyes light up!

USED FOR	SHAPE/ COLOR	NUMBER TO CUT	BLOCK SIZE			
			6"	8"	10"	12"
A		1	1½ x 6½	1¾ x 8½	2 x 10½	2½ x 12½
B		1	2 x 6	2½ x 7¾	3 x 9⅝	3½ x 11½
C		1	2¼	3	3⅝	4¼
D		1	1 x 2¼	1⅛ x 3	1⅜ x 3½	1½ x 4
E		2	1	1⅛	1⅜	1½
F		1	1 x 3¾	1¼ x 5	1⅜ x 6	1½ x 7
G		1	1¼ x 1½	1⅝ x 1⅞	1¾ x 2¼	2 x 2½
H		1	1 x 1¼	1¼ x 1⅝	1⅜ x 1¾	1½ x 2
I		1	1¼ x 6½	1½ x 8½	1¾ x 10½	2 x 12½
J		1	1½ x 6½	1¾ x 8½	2¼ x 10½	2½ x 12½
K		1	2¼ x 4¾	3 x 6	3½ x 7½	4 x 9
L		1	¾ x 1¼	⅞ x 1⅝	⅞ x 1¾	1 x 2
M		1	2¾	3⅝	4¼	5
Wheels and hubcaps ● ○		2*, 2*	See page 10			

*Fuse on after sewing the complete block.

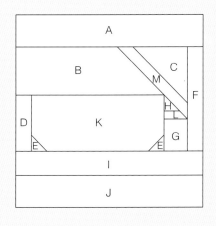

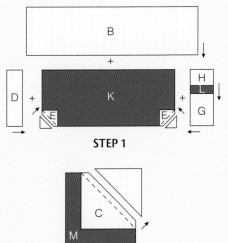

STEP 1

STEP 2

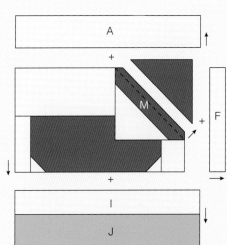

STEP 3

little red wagon 53

twin pines

(Design by Nancy Johnson-Srebro)

Try making each pine tree from different fabrics.

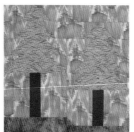

USED FOR	SHAPE/ COLOR	NUMBER TO CUT	BLOCK SIZE			
			6"	8"	10"	12"
A	▭	2 ▭	1¾ X 2½	2⅛ X 3⅛	2½ X 3⅞	3 X 4½
B	◻▭	2 ▭	1¾ X 2⅛	2⅛ X 2⅝	2½ X 3¼	3 X 3¾
C	◺	4 ◻	1¼	1½	1¾	2
D	◹◹	4 ▭	1¼ X 1½	1½ X 1⅞	1¾ X 2⅛	2 X 2½
E	◹◹	4 ▭	1¼ X 1¾	1½ X 2⅛	1¾ X 2⅝	2 X 3
F	◹◹	4 ▭	1¼ X 2	1½ X 2½	1¾ X 3	2 X 3½
G	▭	1 ▭	1¼ X 3½	1½ X 4½	1¾ X 5½	2 X 6½
H	▲	2 ▬	1¼ X 2	1½ X 2½	1¾ X 3	2 X 3½
I	▲	2 ▬	1¼ X 2½	1½ X 3¼	1¾ X 3¾	2 X 4½
J	▲	2 ▬	1¼ X 3	1½ X 3¾	1¾ X 4¾	2 X 5½
K	▲	2 ▬	1¼ X 3½	1½ X 4½	1¾ X 5½	2 X 6½
L	▪	1 ▪	1 X 2½	1¼ X 3⅛	1½ X 3⅞	1½ X 4½
M	▪	1 ▪	1 X 2⅛	1¼ X 2⅝	1½ X 3¼	1½ X 3¾
N	▭	1 ▭	1½ X 3½	1⅞ X 4½	2⅛ X 5½	2½ X 6½
O	◺	1 ◻	⅞	1	1⅛	1¼
P	▭	1 ▭	1⅛ X 3½	1⅜ X 4½	1½ X 5½	1¾ X 6½

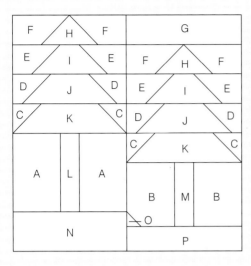

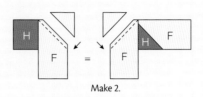

Make 2.

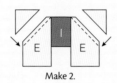

Make 2.

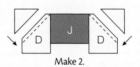

Make 2.

Make 2.

STEP 1

tip

The trees will really stand out if you use different greens. Achieve a similar contrast with the fabric for the trunks.

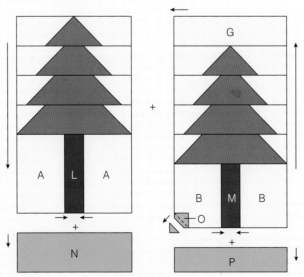

STEP 2

moon rocket

(Design by Cindy Mundy Cochran)

For a nighttime launch, use a dark background fabric and a light colored fabric for the rocket.

USED FOR	SHAPE/ COLOR	NUMBER TO CUT	BLOCK SIZE			
			6"	9"	12"	15"
A		2	2¾ x 6	3⅞ x 8¾	5 x 11½	6⅛ x 14¼
B		2	1¼	1⅝	2	2⅜
C		2	1 x 2¾	1¼ x 3⅞	1½ x 5	1¾ x 6⅛
D		1	1 x 1¼	1¼ x 1⅝	1½ x 2	1¾ x 2⅜
E		1	1⅝ x 2	2⅛ x 2¾	2¾ x 3½	3⅜ x 4¼
F		2	1 x 2⅝	1¼ x 3¾	1½ x 4¾	1¾ x 5¾
G		1	1½ x 2	2 x 2¾	2½ x 3½	3 x 4¼
H		2	2	2¾	3½	4¼
I		1	1 x 2⅝	1¼ x 3¾	1½ x 4¾	1¾ x 5¾
J		2	1 x 2	1¼ x 2¾	1½ x 3½	1¾ x 4¼
K		2	1 x 1¼	1¼ x 1⅝	1½ x 2	1¾ x 2⅜

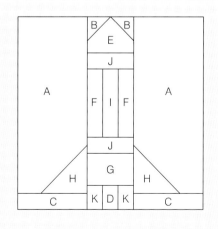

*short side of rectangle E

STEP 1

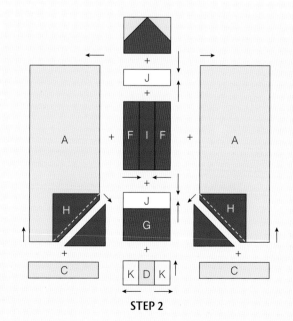

STEP 2

miss lady bug

(Design by Nancy Johnson-Srebro)

This is one bug you'll be happy to see.

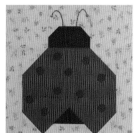

USED FOR	SHAPE/ COLOR	NUMBER TO CUT	BLOCK SIZE			
			6"	8"	10"	12"
A	▫	2 ▫	2½	3¼	3⅞	4½
B	▭	1 ▭	1½ x 2½	1⅞ x 3	2⅛ x 3¾	2½ x 4½
C	◺	2 ▫	1	1⅛	1⅜	1½
D	◹	2 ▫	1¾	2¼	2⅝	3
E	▭	2 ▭	1¼ x 4½	1½ x 5¾	1¾ x 7⅛	2 x 8½
F	◿	2 ▫	1½	1⅞	2¼	2½
G	⬡◺	2 ▭	1 x 1¾	1⅛ x 2⅛	1⅜ x 2½	1½ x 3
H	⬡	2 ▬	2¾ x 4½	3½ x 5¾	4¼ x 7⅛	5 x 8½
I	◣	2 ▬	1¼ x 1¾	1½ x 2⅛	1⅝ x 2½	2 x 3
J	⬠	1 ▬	1½ x 2½	1⅞ x 3	2¼ x 3¾	2½ x 4½
Circles	●	10*	See page 10			

*Fuse on after sewing the complete block.

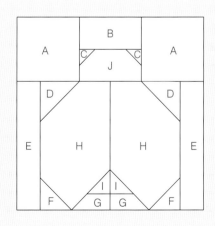

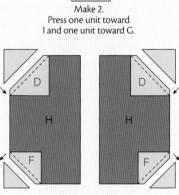

STEP 1

Make 2.
Press one unit toward
I and one unit toward G.

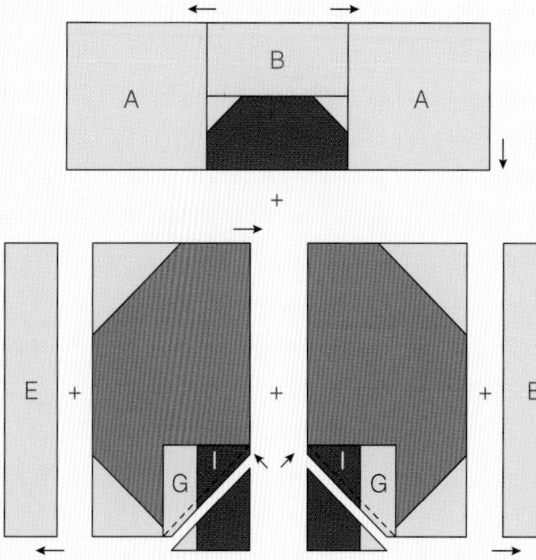

STEP 2

lemonade

(Design by Nancy Johnson-Srebro)

Fill this pitcher and glass with a cool drink. Enjoy!

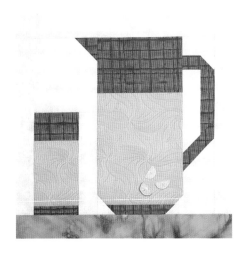

USED FOR	SHAPE/ COLOR	NUMBER TO CUT	BLOCK SIZE			
			6"	8"	10"	12"
A		2	1 X 5¾	1⅛ X 7½	1¼ X 9¼	1½ X 11
B		1	1 X 5½	1⅛ X 7¼	1⅜ X 9	1½ X 10½
C		1	⅞	1	1⅛	1¼
D		1	1 X 1⅜	1⅛ X 1¾	1⅜ X 2	1½ X 2¼
E		1	2¼ X 2½	2¾ X 2⅞	3½ X 3⅞	4 X 4½
F		1	1 X 3¼	1⅛ X 4½	1¼ X 5	1½ X 6
G		1	1 X 2⅞	1¼ X 3½	1⅜ X 4⅛	1½ X 5
H		1	1⅜ X 2⅜	1¾ X 3¼	2 X 3⅞	2¼ X 4½
I		2	1	1¼	1⅜	1½
J		1	1¼ X 6½	1½ X 8½	1¾ X 10½	2 X 12½
K		1	¾ X 1¾	⅞ X 2⅛	⅞ X 2¾	1 X 3
L		1	1¼ X 1¾	1½ X 2⅛	1¾ X 2¾	2 X 3
M		1	2 X 2⅞	2½ X 3¾	3 X 4½	3½ X 5¼
N		1	1⅛	1⅜	1½	1¾
O		1	¾ X 2⅞	⅞ X 3¾	⅞ X 4½	1 X 5¼
P		1	⅞ X 1⅜	1 X 1¾	1⅛ X 2	1¼ X 2¼
Q		1	⅞ X 2⅞	1 X 3½	1⅛ X 4⅛	1¼ X 5
R		1	1⅜ X 1⅞	1¾ X 2½	2 X 2⅞	2¼ X 3¼
S		1	1¾ X 2¼	2⅛ X 3⅛	2¾ X 3⅜	3 X 4
T		1	2⅞ X 3½	3¾ X 4½	4½ X 5½	5¼ X 6½

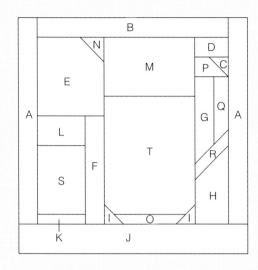

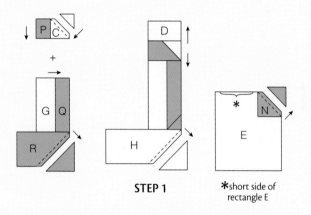

STEP 1

*short side of
rectangle E

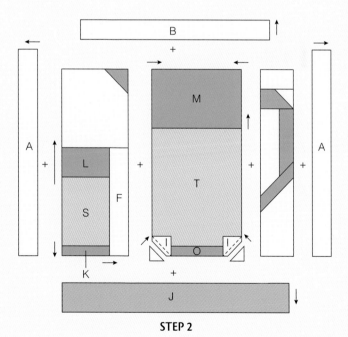

STEP 2

tip

Use fun and funky fabrics
to make whatever drink
you like. Raspberry lemon-
ade is one of my favorites!

pineapple
(Design by Jennifer Srebro)

Try this block in a tropical scene.

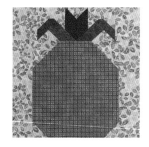

USED FOR	SHAPE/ COLOR	NUMBER TO CUT	BLOCK SIZE			
			6"	8"	10"	12"
A	▭	2 ▭	1¾ X 2	2¼ X 2½	2½ X 3	3 X 3½
B	◿◺	2 ▭	1 X 2¼	1⅛ X 2¾	1⅜ X 3½	1½ X 4
C	◹	8 ☐	1	1⅛	1⅜	1½
D	◹	2 ▭	1½ X 2	1⅞ X 2½	2⅛ X 3	2½ X 3½
E	▭	2 ▭	1½ X 5	1⅞ X 6½	2⅛ X 8	2½ X 9½
F	◺	2 ☐	1¼	1½	1¾	2
G	◿	2 ☐	1¾	2⅛	2⅝	3
H	▱ ▱▱	2 ▭	1 X 2	1⅛ X 2½	1⅜ X 3	1½ X 3½
I	▱ ▱▱	2 ▭	1 X 1½	1⅛ X 1⅞	1⅜ X 2⅛	1½ X 2½
J	▽	2 ▭	1½ X 1¾	1⅞ X 2⅛	2⅛ X 2⅝	2½ X 3
K	⬡	1 ▭	4½ X 5	5¾ X 6½	7¼ X 8	8½ X 9½

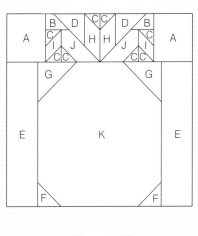

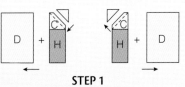

STEP 1

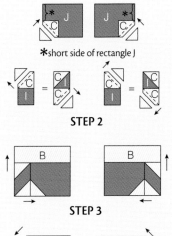

*short side of rectangle J

STEP 2

STEP 3

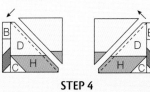

STEP 4

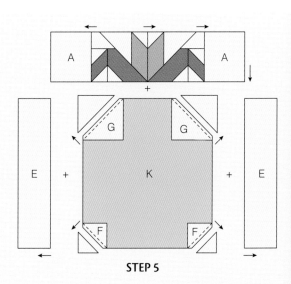

STEP 5

pineapple

stockings for everyone

(Design by Nancy Johnson-Srebro)

Try making the background dark and the stockings light.

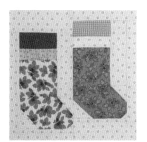

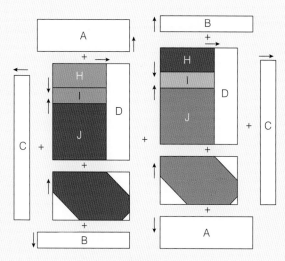

USED FOR	SHAPE/ COLOR	NUMBER TO CUT	BLOCK SIZE			
			6"	8"	10"	12"
A	▭	2 ▭	1½ x 3½	1⅞ x 4½	2⅛ x 5½	2½ x 6½
B	▭	2 ▭	1 x 3½	1⅛ x 4½	1⅜ x 5½	1½ x 6½
C	▭	2 ▭	1 x 5	1⅛ x 6½	1⅜ x 8	1½ x 9½
D	▭	2 ▭	1¼ x 3½	1½ x 4½	1¾ x 5½	2 x 6½
E	◺	2 □	1¼	1½	1¾	2
F	◺	2 □	¾	⅞	⅞	1
G	◺	2 □	1⅜	1⅝	2	2¼
H	▬	1* ▬	1¼ x 2¼	1½ x 2⅞	1¾ x 3⅜	2 x 4
I	▬	1* ▬	1 x 2¼	1⅛ x 2⅞	1⅜ x 3⅜	1½ x 4
J	▬	1* ▬	2¼	2⅞	3⅜	4
K	⬡	1* ▬	2 x 3	2½ x 3⅞	3 x 4⅝	3½ x 5½

*Using different colors, repeat for the second stocking.

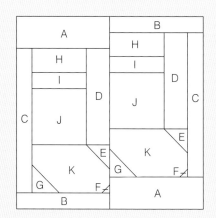

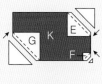

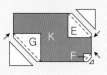

STEP 1

STEP 2

skate away

(Design by Nancy Johnson-Srebro)

Use really funky fabrics for the skate and sock.

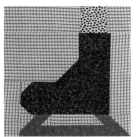

USED FOR	SHAPE/ COLOR	NUMBER TO CUT	BLOCK SIZE			
			6"	8"	10"	12"
A	▭	1 ▭	1¾ x 4⅛	2 x 5¼	2¾ x 6⅜	3 x 7¾
B	▭	1 ▭	1⅝ x 1¾	2 x 2¼	2⅜ x 2¾	2¾ x 3
C	▱	1 ▭	2¾ x 4	3½ x 5	4 x 6¼	5 x 7½
D	▭	1 ▭	1½ x 4¼	2 x 5½	2¼ x 6½	2½ x 8
E	▭	1 ▭	1¼ x 3	1½ x 4	1¾ x 4¾	2 x 5½
F	◺	4 ▢	1	1¼	1⅜	1½
G	◺	1 ▢	1½	2	2¼	2½
H	▭	1 ▭	1 x 2½	1¼ x 2⅝	1⅜ x 3¾	1½ x 4½
I	◺	1 ▢	1¼	1½	1¾	2
J	▱	1 ▭	1 x 2¼	1¼ x 3⅛	1⅜ x 3½	1½ x 4
K	▱	1 ▭	1 x 2	1¼ x 2¾	1⅜ x 3	1½ x 3½
L	▱	1 ▭	1 x 5¾	1¼ x 7½	1⅜ x 9¼	1½ x 11
M	▭	1 ▭	2 x 4¾	2½ x 6	3 x 7½	3½ x 9
N	◣	1 ▪	1½	1⅞	2⅛	2½
O	▭	1 ▪	2 x 2¾	2½ x 3½	3 x 4	3½ x 5
P	▢	1 ▢	1¾	2	2¾	3

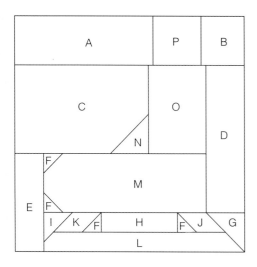

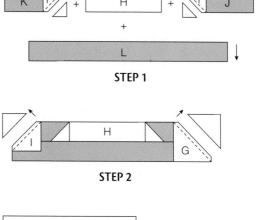

STEP 1

STEP 2

STEP 3

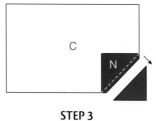

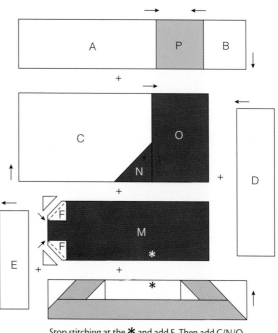

Stop stitching at the ✽ and add E. Then add C/N/O unit. Add D and finish stitching the ✽ seam.

STEP 4

snowflake

(Design by Arlene Begey Shea)

For a different look, make the snowflake dark and the background light.

USED FOR	SHAPE/ COLOR	NUMBER TO CUT	BLOCK SIZE			
			6"	8"	10"	12"
A		8	1⅝ X 2⅞	2 X 3⅝	2½ X 4⅝	2¾ X 5¼
B		8	1¼ X 2⅞	1⅜ X 3⅝	1⅞ X 4⅝	2 X 5¼
C		12	1	1¼	1¼	1½
D		4	2	2½	3	3½
E		8	1 X 2⅞	1¼ X 3⅝	1¼ X 4⅝	1½ X 5¼
F		4	3¼	4⅛	5⅛	6
G		2	1 X 2¾	1¼ X 3⅜	1¼ X 4⅜	1½ X 5
H		1	1 X 5½	1¼ X 7	1¼ X 9	1½ X 10½

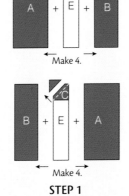

STEP 1

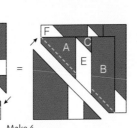

Make 4.

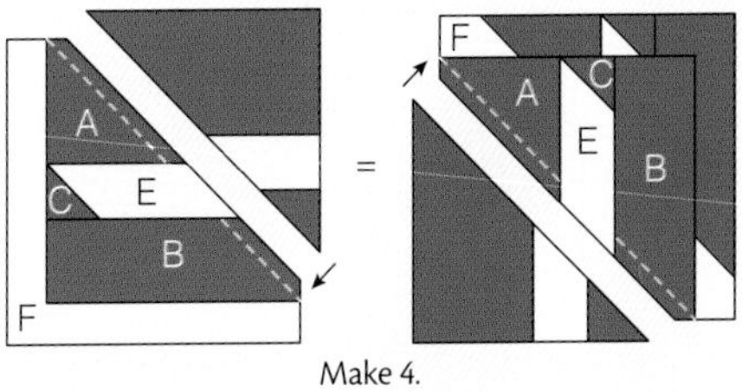

STEP 2

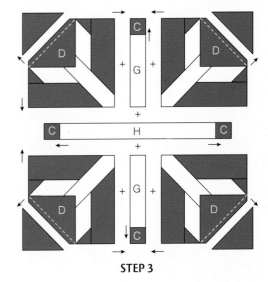

STEP 3

shooting star

(Design by Karen F. Srebro)

Use several of these blocks to light up the sky!

USED FOR	SHAPE/ COLOR	NUMBER TO CUT	BLOCK SIZE				
			4"	6"	8"	10"	12"
A		4	1¼	1½	1¾	2¼	2½
B		4	1¼ X 1⅜	1½ X 1¾	1¾ X 2⅛	2¼ X 2½	2½ X 3
C		1	1½	2	2½	3	3½
D		2	1½ X 2	2 X 3	2½ X 4	3 X 4½	3½ X 5½
E		1	2	3	4	4½	5½
F		4	1¼ X 1½	1½ X 2	1¾ X 2½	2¼ X 3	2½ X 3½
G		4	1¼ X 1⅞	1½ X 2¾	1¾ X 3⅝	2¼ X 4¼	2½ X 5
H		1	2	2½	3	4	4½

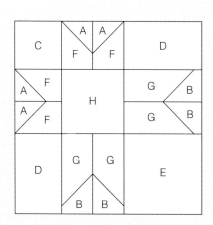

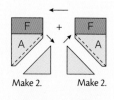

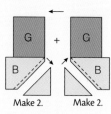

STEP 1

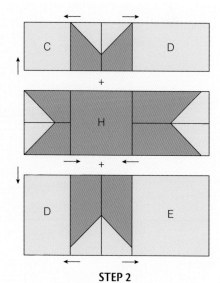

STEP 2

log cabin
(Design by Nancy Johnson-Srebro)

Have fun making this log cabin look country or contemporary.

USED FOR	SHAPE/ COLOR	NUMBER TO CUT	BLOCK SIZE			
			6"	9"	12"	15"
A	▭	1 ▭	1¼ x 1½	1⅝ x 2	2 x 2½	2⅜ x 3
B	▱	1 ▭	1½ x 4½	2 x 6½	2½ x 8½	3 x 10½
C	▭	1 ▭	1½ x 2½	2 x 3½	2½ x 4½	3 x 5½
D	△▭	3 ▭	1 x 2½	1¼ x 3½	1½ x 4½	1¾ x 5½
E	▭	6 ▭	1	1¼	1½	1¾
F	▭	1 ▭	1 x 3½	1¼ x 5	1½ x 6½	1¾ x 8
G	▭	3 ▭	1 x 1½	1¼ x 2	1½ x 2½	1¾ x 3
H	▭	3 ▭	1 x 3½	1¼ x 5	1½ x 6½	1¾ x 8
I	▭	2 ▭	1 x 1½	1¼ x 2	1½ x 2½	1¾ x 3
J	▪	4 ▪	1	1¼	1½	1¾
K	◿▭	2 ▭	1 x 2½	1¼ x 3½	1½ x 4½	1¾ x 5½
L	▢	1 ▢	1½	2	2½	3
M	▢	2 ▢	1	1¼	1½	1¾
N	▭	1 ▭	1¼ x 6½	1⅝ x 9½	2 x 12½	2⅜ x 15½
O	▭	2 ▭	1 x 5	1¼ x 7¼	1½ x 9½	1¾ x 11¾
P	◺	2 ▢	1½	2	2½	3
Q	▭	1 ▭	1¼ x 3¾	1⅝ x 5⅜	2 x 7	2⅜ x 8⅝
R	▭	1 ▭	1¼ x 2¼	1⅝ x 3⅛	2 x 4	2⅜ x 4⅞

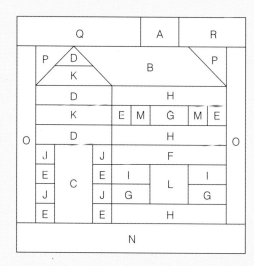

tip

To create your own home, use wood-grain print fabrics, plaids, and stripes. Embellish with some shrubs.

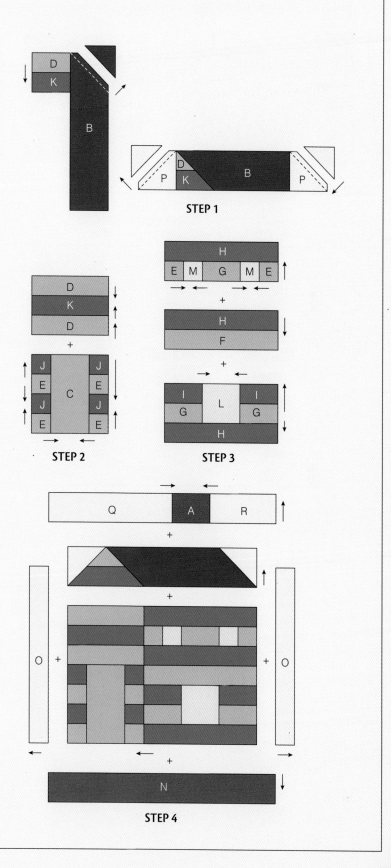

STEP 1

STEP 2

STEP 3

STEP 4

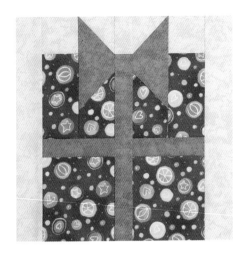

all tied up

(Design by Nancy Johnson-Srebro)

Dig out all those fun fabrics and make a wedding, birthday, or Christmas present.

USED FOR	SHAPE/ COLOR	NUMBER TO CUT	BLOCK SIZE			
			6"	8"	10"	12"
A	▭	2 ▭	1¼ x 6½	1⅜ x 8½	1⅞ x 10½	2 x 12½
B	▢ ◹	4 ▢	1½	1⅞	2⅛	2½
C	▭	1 ▭	1 x 1½	1¼ x 1⅞	1¼ x 2⅛	1½ x 2½
D	▬	2 ▬	1½ x 2¾	1⅞ x 3⅜	2⅛ x 4⅜	2½ x 5
E	◣◥	2 ▬	1½ x 2¼	1⅞ x 2⅝	2⅛ x 3⅝	2½ x 4
F	▬	2 ▬	2½ x 2¾	3¼ x 3½	3¾ x 4¼	4½ x 5
G	▱	2 ▱	1 x 2½	1¼ x 3¼	1¼ x 3¾	1½ x 4½
H	▬	1 ▬	1 x 5	1¼ x 6⅜	1¼ x 8⅛	1½ x 9½
I	▪	1 ▪	1	1¼	1¼	1½
J	◣	2 ▬	1½ x 3	1⅞ x 4	2⅛ x 4½	2½ x 5½

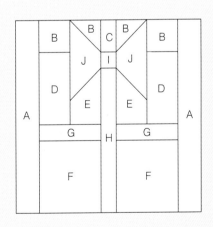

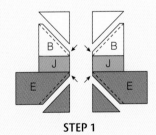

STEP 1

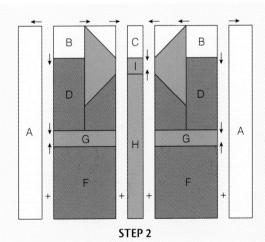

STEP 2

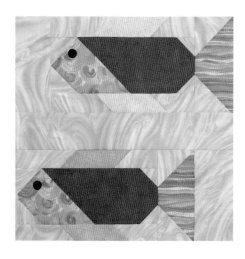

swimmin' fish

(Design by Nancy Johnson-Srebro)

To add some variety, use different fabrics for each fish.

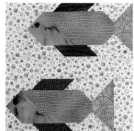
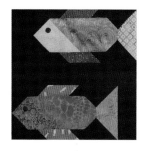

USED FOR	SHAPE/ COLOR	NUMBER TO CUT	BLOCK SIZE			
			6"	8"	10"	12"
A	▭	2 ▭	1½ X 3	1⅞ X 3¾	2⅛ X 4¾	2½ X 5½
B	◸	4 ▫	1¼	1½	1¾	2
C	◹	4 ▫	1	1¼	1¼	1½
D	▱▱	4 ▭	1 X 2¼	1⅛ X 2⅞	1⅜ X 3½	1½ X 4
E	▱▱	4 ▭	1 X 2	1⅛ X 2⅛	1⅜ X 2½	1½ X 3
F	◺	4 ▫	1½	1⅞	2⅛	2½
G	▭	1 ▭	1½ X 6½	2 X 8½	2 X 10½	2½ X 12½
H	⬟	2 ▬	2 X 3¾	2½ X 4¾	3 X 6	3½ X 7
I	▱▱	2*	1 X 2¼	1⅛ X 3	1⅜ X 4	1½ X 4½
J	▽	2 ▬	1½ X 3	1⅞ X 3¾	2⅛ X 4¾	2½ X 5½
K	⬠	2 ▬	2 X 2¾	2½ X 3½	3 X 4¼	3½ X 5
Eyes	●	2**	See page 10			

*Using different colors, repeat for the other fish. **Fuse on after sewing the complete block.

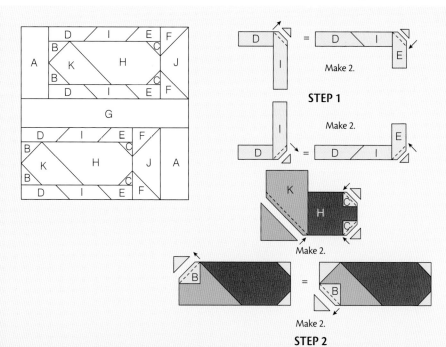

STEP 1

Make 2.

STEP 2

Make 2.

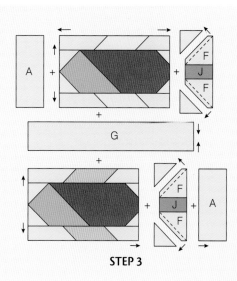

STEP 3

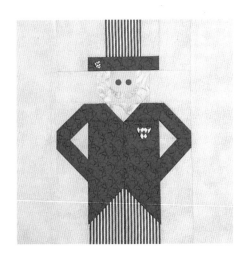

uncle sam

(Design by Arlene Begey Shea)

A fun patriotic block.

  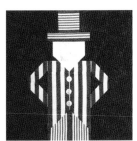

USED FOR	SHAPE/ COLOR	NUMBER TO CUT	BLOCK SIZE			
			6"	9"	12"	15"
A	▭	2 ▭	1⅝ X 6½	2¼ X 9½	2¾ X 12½	3⅜ X 15½
B	▭	2 ▭	1⅜ X 1⅞	1¾ X 2⅝	2¼ X 3¼	2⅝ X 4
C	▭	2 ▭	1 X 1½	1¼ X 2	1½ X 2½	1¾ X 3
D	◹	2 ▢	¾	⅞	1	1⅛
E	▭	2 ▭	1⅜ X 1⅝	1⅞ X 2	2¼ X 2¾	2⅝ X 3¼
F	◺	4 ▢	1	1¼	1½	1¾
G	◱◲	2 ▭	1⅜ X 3	1¾ X 4¼	2¼ X 5½	2⅝ X 6⅞
H	◺	2 ▢	1¼	1⅝	2	2¼
I	◢◣	2 ▮	1½ X 2	2 X 2¾	2½ X 3½	3 X 4¼
J	▪	1 ▪	1½	2	2½	3
K	▬	1 ▬	⅞ X 2½	1⅛ X 3½	1¼ X 4½	1½ X 5½
L	◣◢	2 ▮	1 X 1½	1⅜ X 2	1½ X 2½	1¾ X 3
M	◣◢	2 ▮	1½ X 3¼	2 X 4⅜	2½ X 6	3 X 7⅜
N	⬡	2 ▮	1⅜ X 1½	1¾ X 2	2¼ X 2½	2⅝ X 2⅞
O	⬡	2 ▮	1⅜ X 1⅝	1¾ X 2	2¼ X 2¾	2⅝ X 3¼
P	▱	2 ▱	⅞ X 1⅜	1⅛ X 1⅞	1¼ X 2¼	1½ X 2⅝
Q	▽	1 ▭	1 X 1½	1⅜ X 2¼	1½ X 2½	1¾ X 3
R	▭	1 ▭	1¼ X 1⅜	1¾ X 1⅞	2 X 2¼	2¼ X 2⅝
Eyes and Mustache ● ◡		2*, 2*	See page 10			

*Fuse on after sewing the complete block.

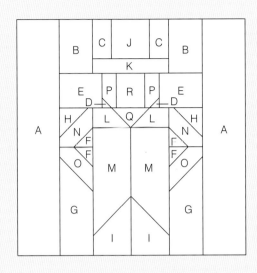

Dress up this guy with buttons and add a flag and sparklers. Great for an Independence Day or patriotic theme!

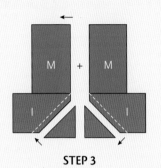

STEP 3

N

✳short side of rectangle N

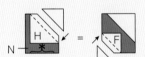

N

✳short side of rectangle N

STEP 1

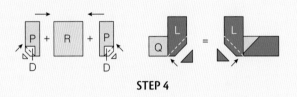

STEP 4

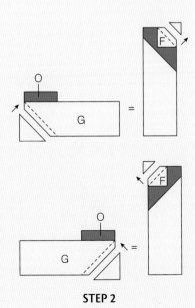

STEP 2

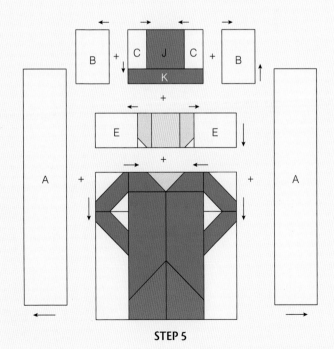

STEP 5

runabout

(Design by Nancy Johnson-Srebro)

How many of you fondly remember your first car?

USED FOR	SHAPE/ COLOR	NUMBER TO CUT	BLOCK SIZE			
			6"	8"	10"	12"
A	▭	1 ▭	1¾ x 6½	2⅛ x 8½	2¾ x 10½	3 x 12½
B	▱	1 ▭	1¾ x 2¼	2¼ x 2¾	2½ x 3½	3 x 4
C	◣	1 ▭	1¾ x 3	2¼ x 4⅛	2½ x 4⅜	3 x 5½
D	▭	1 ▭	1¼ x 6½	1½ x 8½	1¾ x 10½	2 x 12½
E	◿	3 ▭	⅞	1	1⅛	1¼
F	▭	1 ▭	1¾ x 6½	2⅛ x 8½	2½ x 10½	3 x 12½
G	▭	1 ▭	2 x 6½	2½ x 8½	3 x 10½	3½ x 12½
H	◢	1 ▭	1 x 2¾	1¼ x 3½	1¼ x 4¼	1½ x 5
I	▱	1 ▭	1¼ x 1⅝	1½ x 2	1¾ x 2⅜	2 x 2¾
J	▱	1 ▭	1 x 1¾	1⅛ x 2¼	1⅜ x 2½	1½ x 3
K	▱	1 ▭	1¾ x 2	2¼ x 2½	2½ x 3	3 x 3½
L	◿	1 ▭	1¼	1½	1¾	2
M	▱	1 ▭	1¼ x 2⅜	1½ x 3	1¾ x 3⅝	2 x 4¼
Wheels and hub caps ⬤●		2*, 2*	See page 10			

*Fuse on after sewing the complete block.

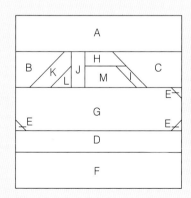
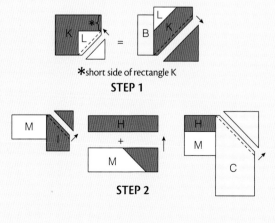
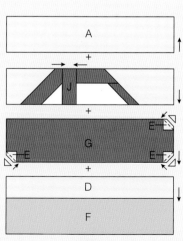

* short side of rectangle K
STEP 1

STEP 2

STEP 3

misty the dog

(Design by Nancy Johnson-Srebro)

Have fun finding furry-looking fabric for this little pup.

USED FOR	SHAPE/ COLOR	NUMBER TO CUT	BLOCK SIZE			
			6"	9"	12"	15"
A		1	2½ x 3¼	3½ x 4⅝	4½ x 6	5½ x 7⅜
B		1	2¼	3⅛	4	4⅞
C		9	¾	⅞	1	1⅛
D		3	1	1¼	1½	1¾
E		1	1 x 2½	1¼ x 3½	1½ x 4½	1¾ x 5½
F		2	1 x 1¾	1¼ x 2⅜	1½ x 3	1¾ x 3⅝
G		1	1¾ x 4½	2⅜ x 6½	3 x 8½	3⅝ x 10½
H		1	1½ x 4½	2 x 6½	2½ x 8½	3 x 10½
I		2	1 x 1¾	1¼ x 2⅜	1½ x 3	1¾ x 3⅝
J		1	1½	2	2½	3
K		1	2¾ x 4¼	3⅞ x 6⅛	5 x 8	6⅛ x 9⅞
L		2	1 x 2	1¼ x 2¾	1½ x 3½	1¾ x 4¼
M		1	2¼ x 2½	3⅛ x 3½	4 x 4½	4⅞ x 5½
N		2	1 x 1½	1¼ x 2	1½ x 2½	1¾ x 3
O		1	1¼	1⅝	2	2⅜
Eyes and nose ● ▼		2*, 1*	See page 10			

*Fuse on after sewing the complete block.

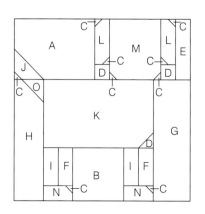
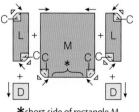
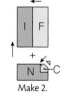
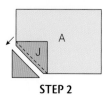

*short side of rectangle M
STEP 1

Make 2.

STEP 2

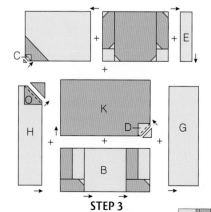

STEP 3

mikey moose

(Design by Jennifer Srebro)

If you ever see a moose, you'll be surprised at the size of its antlers.

USED FOR	SHAPE/ COLOR	NUMBER TO CUT	BLOCK SIZE			
			6"	8"	10"	12"
A		1	2¼ X 3	2⅞ X 3⅞	3⅜ X 4¾	4 X 5½
B		1	2¼ X 2½	2⅞ X 3¼	3⅜ X 3⅝	4 X 4½
C		1	1 X 2¼	1⅛ X 2⅞	1⅜ X 3⅜	1½ X 4
D		1	1 X 2½	1⅛ X 3⅛	1⅜ X 3⅞	1½ X 4½
E		1	2¾ X 3	3½ X 4	4¼ X 4½	5 X 5½
F		4	1	1⅛	1⅜	1½
G		2	1 X 1¾	1⅛ X 2⅛	1⅜ X 2⅝	1½ X 3
H		1	1¼ X 2¾	1½ X 3⅜	1¾ X 4⅜	2 X 5
I		1	¾	⅞	⅞	1
J		3	1¼	1½	1¾	2
K		2	1 X 1¼	1⅛ X 1½	1⅜ X 1¾	1½ X 2
L		1	1 X 4	1⅛ X 5	1⅜ X 6½	1½ X 7½
M		1	1 X 2¼	1⅛ X 2⅞	1⅜ X 3⅜	1½ X 4
N		1	1¼ X 2¼	1½ X 2⅞	1¾ X 3⅜	2 X 4
O		2	1 X 2	1⅛ X 2½	1⅜ X 3	1½ X 3½
P		1	1¼ X 1¾	1½ X 2¼	1¾ X 2½	2 X 3
Q		1	1 X 1¾	1⅛ X 2¼	1⅜ X 2½	1½ X 3
R		1	2½ X 3¾	3⅛ X 5	3⅞ X 5¾	4½ X 7
S		1	1¾ X 2¼	2⅛ X 2¾	2⅝ X 3½	3 X 4
T		2	1	1⅛	1⅜	1½
U		1	1¼	1½	1¾	2
V		2	1 X 2¼	1⅛ X 2⅞	1⅜ X 3⅜	1½ X 4

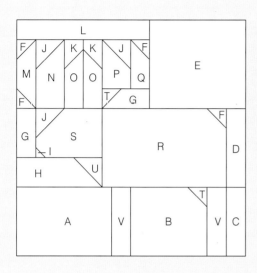

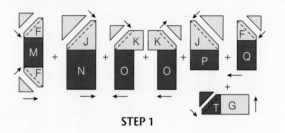

STEP 1

STEP 2

STEP 3

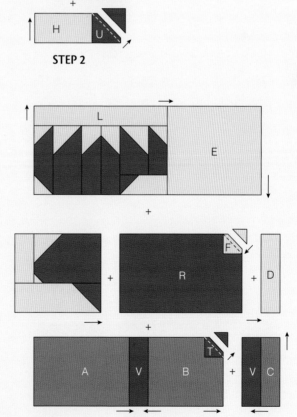

tip

Make Mikey really stand out by using the same fabric for both the grass and sky. He's an imposing sight!

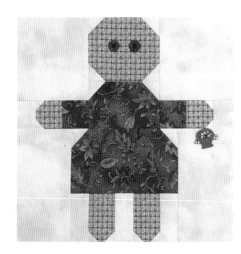

rag doll

(Design by Nancy Johnson-Srebro)

Many fond memories come to mind when I think of my old rag doll.

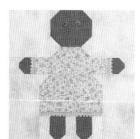

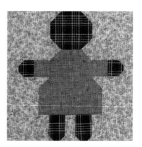

USED FOR	SHAPE/ COLOR	NUMBER TO CUT	BLOCK SIZE			
			6"	9"	12"	15"
A	▭	2 ▭	2½ x 2¾	3½ x 3⅞	4½ x 5	5½ x 6⅛
B	▭	2 ▭	1 x 1¼	1¼ x 1⅝	1½ x 2	1¾ x 2⅜
C	◺	8 □	1	1¼	1½	1¾
D	◹	8 □	¾	⅞	1	1⅛
E	▭	2 ▭	2 x 3½	2¾ x 5	3½ x 6½	4¼ x 8
F	▭	3 ▭	1 x 1¾	1¼ x 2¼	1½ x 3	1¾ x 3½
G	⬡	1 ▭	2¼ x 2½	3⅛ x 3½	4 x 4½	4⅞ x 5½
H	◖	2 ▢	1¼	1⅝	2	2⅜
I	▱	2 ▭	1¼ x 1¾	1⅝ x 2¼	2 x 3	2⅜ x 3½
J	⬠	1 ▭	1¾ x 2½	2⅜ x 3½	3 x 4½	3⅝ x 5½
K	▪	2 ▪	1¼	1⅝	2	2⅜
L	⬡	1 ▭	2¼ x 3½	3¼ x 5	4 x 6½	5 x 8
Eyes	●	2*	See page 10			

*Fuse on after sewing the complete block.

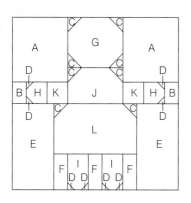

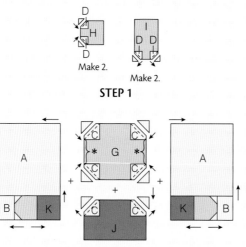

STEP 1

*short side of rectangle G

STEP 2

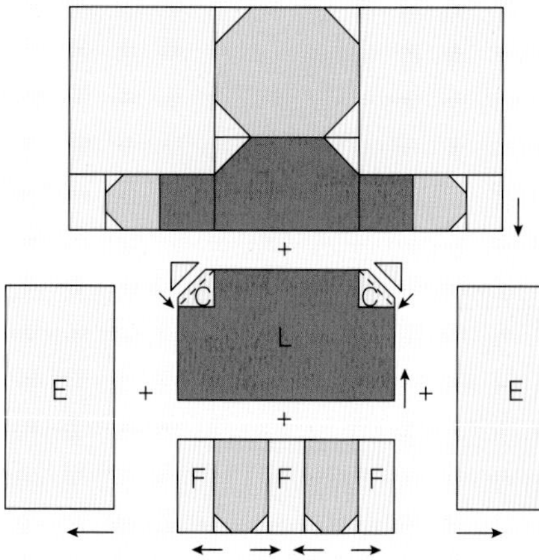

STEP 3

next door neighbor
(Design by Nancy Johnson-Srebro)

Construct the houses in any colors you like because the neighbors won't mind.

USED FOR	SHAPE/ COLOR	NUMBER TO CUT	BLOCK SIZE			
			6"	9"	12"	15"
A		1	1⅛ x 6½	1½ x 9½	1¾ x 12½	2 x 15½
B		2*	1 x 3¾	1¼ x 5½	1½ x 7	1¾ x 8¾
C		1*	1¼ x 1¾	1⅝ x 2⅜	2 x 3	2⅜ x 3⅝
D		1*	1 x 1⅝	1¼ x 2½	1½ x 2¾	1¾ x 3½
E		1*	1⅛ x 2½	1¼ x 3½	1¾ x 4½	2 x 5½
F		1*	1 x 1¼	1¼ x 1⅝	1½ x 2	1¾ x 2⅜
G		1*	1⅛ x 3½	1¼ x 5	1¾ x 6½	2 x 8
H		1*	1¼ x 2⅜	1⅝ x 3⅝	2 x 4¼	2⅜ x 5⅜
I		1*	1¼ x 1⅝	1⅝ x 2½	2 x 2¾	2⅜ x 3½
J		2*	1¼	1⅝	2	2⅜
K	▲	1*	2 x 3½	2¾ x 5	3½ x 6½	4¼ x 8
L	◺	4	2	2¾	3½	4¼

* Using different colors, repeat the cutting for the other house.

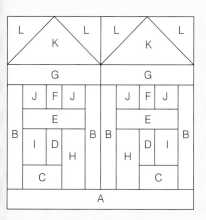

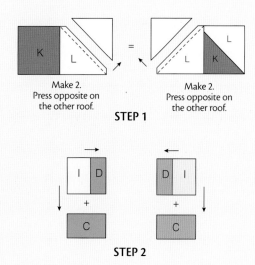

STEP 1

Make 2.
Press opposite on the other roof.

Make 2.
Press opposite on the other roof.

STEP 2

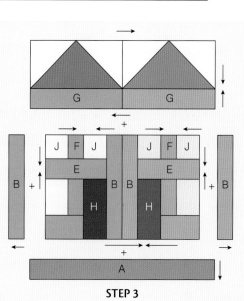

STEP 3

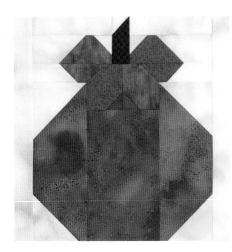

strawberry

(Design by Jennifer Srebro)

I love to go strawberry pickin'. Sometimes I eat as many as I pick!

USED FOR	SHAPE/ COLOR	NUMBER TO CUT	BLOCK SIZE			
			6"	8"	10"	12"
A		2	1 x 6½	1⅛ x 8½	1⅜ x 10½	1½ x 12½
B		2	1¾	2⅛	2½	3
C		2	2 x 2½	2½ x 3⅛	3 x 3⅞	3½ x 4½
D		2	1 x 1¾	1⅛ x 2⅛	1⅜ x 2⅝	1½ x 3
E		2	1¼ x 2	1½ x 2½	1⅞ x 3⅛	2 x 3½
F		3	1	1¼	1¼	1½
G		2	1 x 2¾	1¼ x 3½	1¼ x 4¼	1½ x 5
H		1*	1¼ x 2	1½ x 2½	1⅞ x 3	2 x 3½
I		1*	1 x 1¾	1⅛ x 2⅛	1⅜ x 2⅝	1½ x 3
J		1*	1½ x 1¾	1⅞ x 2⅛	2⅛ x 2½	2½ x 3
K		2	2 x 5¼	2½ x 6¾	3 x 8⅜	3½ x 10
L		2	1	1⅛	1⅜	1½
M		1	2½ x 4	3¼ x 5⅛	3¾ x 6⅜	4½ x 7½
N		1	1 x 1¾	1¼ x 2¼	1¼ x 2⅝	1½ x 3

*Repeat using a different color.

tip

Jewel-tone fabrics give this strawberry a mouth-watering look. Use a variety of reds for a country wallhanging.

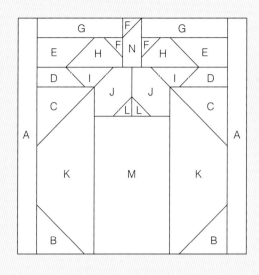

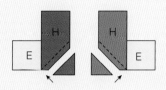

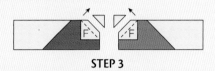

STEP 3

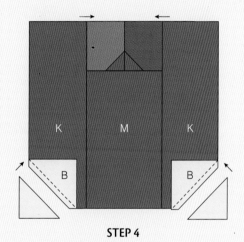

STEP 4

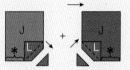

✱short side of rectangle J

STEP 1

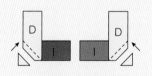

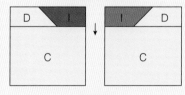

STEP 2

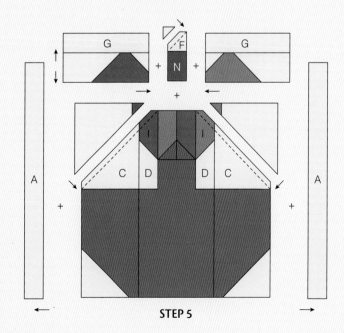

STEP 5

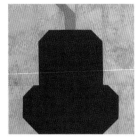

pear
(Design by Jennifer Srebro)

Did you know that some pears are red?

USED FOR	SHAPE/ COLOR	NUMBER TO CUT	BLOCK SIZE			
			6"	8"	10"	12"
A		2	2 x 4¼	2½ x 5½	3 x 6¾	3½ x 8
B		2	1¾	2⅛	2½	3
C		5	1	1¼	1½	1½
D		2	1¼ x 2¾	1½ x 3½	1¾ x 4¼	2 x 5
E		2	1¼	1½	1¾	2
F		1	2¾ x 5	3½ x 6½	4¼ x 8	5 x 9½
G		1	3 x 3½	3⅞ x 4½	4¾ x 5½	5½ x 6½
H		1	1 x 1¾	1¼ x 2⅛	1½ x 2½	1½ x 3
I		1	1	1¼	1½	1½

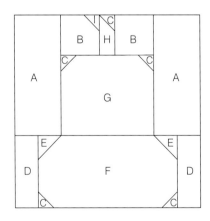

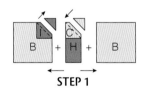

STEP 1

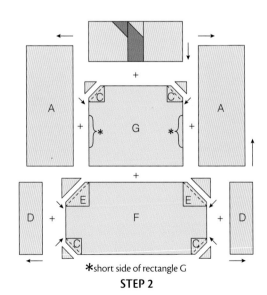

*short side of rectangle G

STEP 2

maple tree

(Design by Janet McCarroll)

Try making the H pieces green and the rest of the tree from reds, yellows, and oranges.

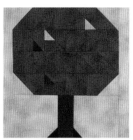

USED FOR	SHAPE/ COLOR	NUMBER TO CUT	BLOCK SIZE			
			6"	9"	12"	15"
A		2	1 x 6½	1¼ x 9½	1½ x 12½	1¾ x 15½
B		4	1½	2	2½	3
C		2	2½ x 2⅝	3½ x 3¾	4½ x 4¾	5½ x 5¾
D		1	1¼ x 2½	1½ x 3½	2 x 4½	2½ x 5½
E		2	1	1¼	1½	1¾
F		18	1½	2	2½	3
G		16	1 x 1½	1¼ x 2	1½ x 2½	1¾ x 3
H		12*	1 x 1½	1¼ x 2	1½ x 2½	1¾ x 3

*Use a variety of colors.

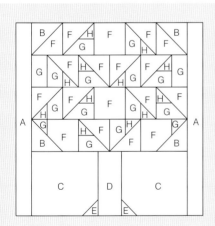

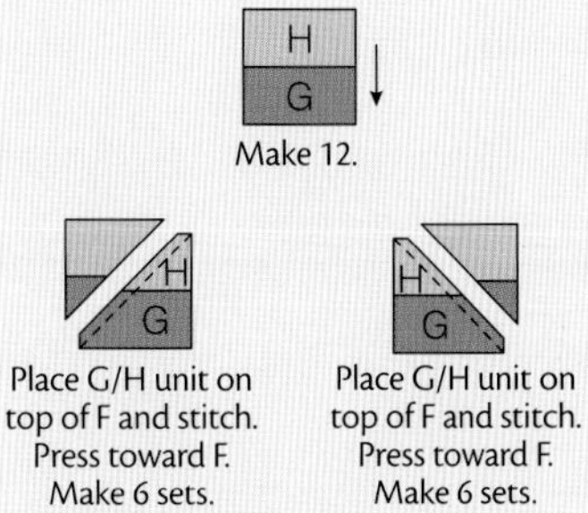

STEP 1

H / G
Make 12.

Place G/H unit on top of F and stitch. Press toward F. Make 6 sets.

Place G/H unit on top of F and stitch. Press toward F. Make 6 sets.

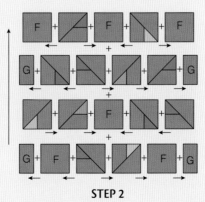

STEP 2

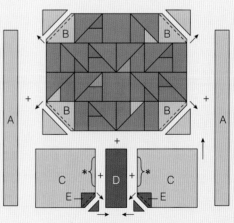

STEP 3

*short side of rectangle C

percolator
(Design by Janet McCarroll)

This beloved coffee pot came in many different colors.

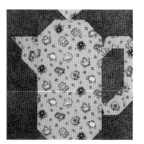

USED FOR	SHAPE/ COLOR	NUMBER TO CUT	BLOCK SIZE			
			6"	9"	12"	15"
A	▭	3 ▭	1¾ x 2	2½ x 2¾	3 x 3½	3 ⅝ x 4¼
B	▭	1 ▭	2 x 3½	2¾ x 4⅞	3½ x 6½	4¼ x 8
C	▱	1 ▭	1¼ x 2¼	1 ⅝ x 3⅛	2 x 4	2⅜ x 4⅞
D	◺	3 ▢	1¼	1⅝	2	2⅜
E	◺◹	2 ▭	1 x 1⅞	1⅜ x 2½	1½ x 3¼	1¾ x 4
F	◺	2 ▢	1	1¼	1½	1¾
G	▱	1 ▭	1½ x 3	2 x 4⅛	2½ x 5½	3 x 6⅞
H	◺	1 ▢	1½	2	2½	3
I	◺	2 ▢	¾	⅞	1	1⅛
J	▽	1 ▭	1 x 1¾	1⅜ x 2¾	1½ x 3	1¾ x 3½
K	△	1 ▭	1¼ x 3½	1 ⅝ x 5	2 x 6½	2⅜ x 8
L	⬠	1 ▭	3½ x 5¼	5 x 7½	6½ x 10	8 x 12⅜
M	◢	1 ▭	1¼ x 2¼	1 ⅝ x 3⅛	2 x 4	2⅜ x 4⅞
N	⬡	1 ▭	1 x 2	1¼ x 2¾	1½ x 3½	1¾ x 4¼
O	◺	2 ▪	1	1¼	1½	1¾
P	◣	1 ▭	1 x 3½	1¼ x 4¾	1½ x 6½	1¾ x 8
Q	▽	1 ▭	1½ x 1¾	2 x 2¼	2½ x 3	3 x 3½
R	◺	1 ▪	¾ x 1½	⅞ x 2	1 x 2½	1⅛ x 3

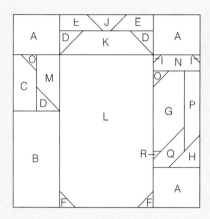

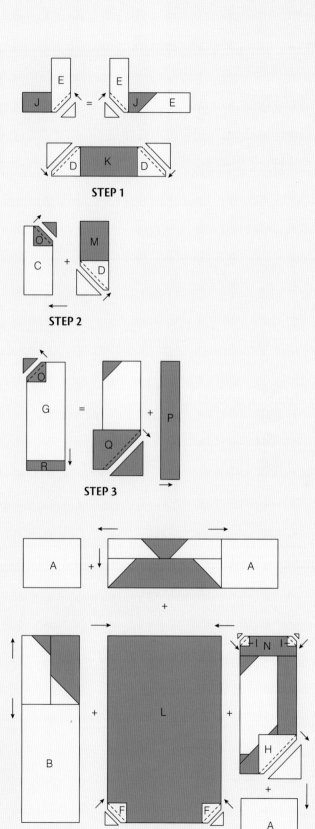

STEP 1

STEP 2

STEP 3

STEP 4

tip

There's been a resurgence in the use of these percolators. Use large-print fabrics for a contemporary look or blue with speckles for the traditional version.

lighthouse
(Design by Cindy Mundy Cochran)

The background will set the tone for this block.

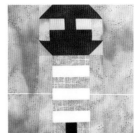

USED FOR	SHAPE/ COLOR	NUMBER TO CUT	BLOCK SIZE			
			6"	9"	12"	15"
A	▬	2 ▬	2 x 6½	2¾ x 9½	3½ x 12½	4¼ x 15½
B	▬	2 ▬	1⅛ x 4¼	1⅜ x 6¼	1¾ x 8	2 x 10
C	◣	4 ◻	1⅛	1⅜	1¾	2
D	▬	2 ▬	1 x 1½	1¼ x 2	1½ x 2½	1¾ x 3
E	▭	2 ▭	1 x 1¼	1¼ x 1⅝	1½ x 2	1¾ x 2⅜
F	▼	2 ▬	1⅛ x 3½	1⅜ x 5	1¾ x 6½	2 x 8
G	▬	1 ▬	1 x 2½	1¼ x 3½	1½ x 4½	1¾ x 5½
H	■	1 ■	1	1¼	1½	1¾
I	▬	3 ▬	1 x 2¼	1¼ x 3¼	1½ x 4	1¾ x 5
J	▭	3 ▭	1 x 2¼	1¼ x 3¼	1½ x 4	1¾ x 5
K	▭	2 ▭	1⅛ x 1¼	1½ x 1¾	1¾ x 2	2⅛ x 2½
L	▬	1 ▬	1 x 1¼	1¼ x 1¾	1½ x 2	1¾ x 2½

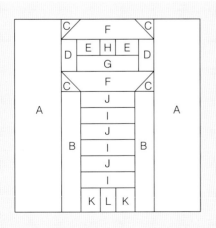

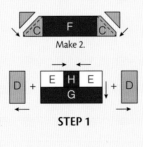

Make 2.

STEP 1

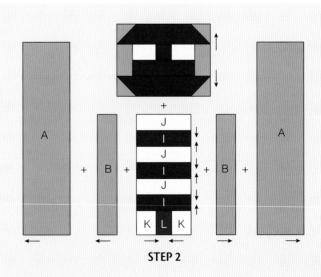

STEP 2

miss scarecrow
(Design by Nancy Johnson-Srebro)

Don't make this missy too pretty or the birds won't be scared!

USED FOR	SHAPE/ COLOR	NUMBER TO CUT	BLOCK SIZE			
			6"	9"	12"	15"
A		2	2 x 2¼	2¾ x 3⅛	3½ x 4	4¼ x 4⅞
B		2	2 x 4½	2¾ x 6½	3½ x 8½	4¼ x 10½
C		8	1	1¼	1½	1¾
D		2	1 x 1½	1¼ x 2	1½ x 2½	1¾ x 3
E		2	1½	2	2½	3
F		2	1¾	2⅜	3	3⅝
G		1	2½ x 3½	3½ x 5	4½ x 6½	5½ x 8
H		1	1¾ x 2½	2⅜ x 3½	3 x 4½	3⅝ x 5½
I		2	1 x 1¼	1¼ x 1⅝	1½ x 2	1¾ x 2⅜
J		1	1	1¼	1½	1¾
K		2	1 x 2	1¼ x 2¾	1½ x 3½	1¾ x 4¼
L		1	1 x 1¾	1¼ x 2⅜	1½ x 3	1¾ x 3⅝
M		1	1 x 3	1¼ x 4¼	1½ x 5½	1¾ x 6¾
N		1	1 x 2	1¼ x 2¾	1½ x 3½	1¾ x 4¼

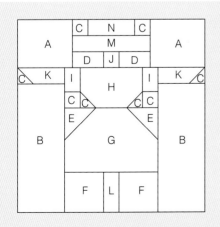

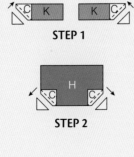

STEP 1

STEP 2

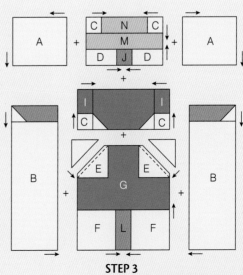

STEP 3

rudolph

(Design by Nancy Johnson-Srebro)

This Rudolph will lead Santa straight to your house!

 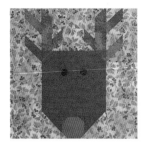 

USED FOR	SHAPE/ COLOR	NUMBER TO CUT	BLOCK SIZE			
			6"	9"	12"	15"
A		2	2 X 4	2¾ X 5¾	3½ X 7½	4¼ X 9¼
B		2	1¾	2⅜	3	3⅝
C		2	1¼ X 3	1⅝ X 4¼	2 X 5½	2⅜ X 6¾
D		6	1	1¼	1½	1¾
E		1	1½	2	2½	3
F		8	1¼	1⅝	2	2⅜
G		1	1½ X 2½	2 X 3½	2½ X 4½	3 X 5½
H		2	1 X 2½	1¼ X 3½	1½ X 4½	1¾ X 5½
I		4	1¼ X 1¾	1⅝ X 2⅜	2 X 3	2⅜ X 3⅝
J		2	1 X 1½	1¼ X 2	1½ X 2½	1¾ X 3
K		2	1	1¼	1½	1¾
L		2	¾	⅞	1	1⅛
M		1	3½	5	6½	8
N		2	1½	2	2½	3
O		1	1½	2	2½	3
Eyes	●	2*	See page 10			

*Fuse on after sewing the complete block.

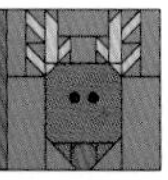

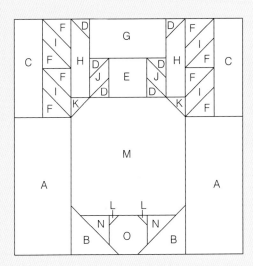

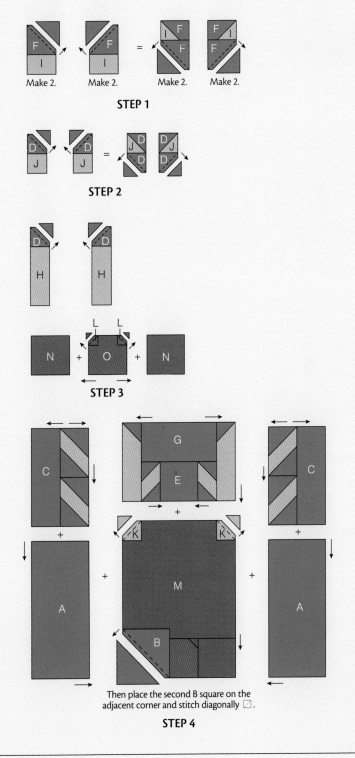

Make 2.   Make 2.   =   Make 2.   Make 2.

STEP 1

STEP 2

STEP 3

Then place the second B square on the adjacent corner and stitch diagonally ⊡.

STEP 4

wheelbarrow

(Design by Nancy Johnson-Srebro)

Fill this wheelbarrow with dirt, rocks, or sand and get ready to work!

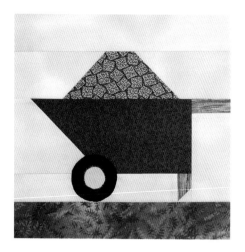

USED FOR	SHAPE/ COLOR	NUMBER TO CUT	BLOCK SIZE			
			6"	8"	10"	12"
A	▭	1	1½ x 6½	1⅞ x 8½	2⅛ x 10½	2½ x 12½
B	◹◺	2	1¾ x 3⅛	2⅛ x 4	2½ x 4⅞	3 x 5¾
C	◿	1	2½ x 3	3⅛ x 3⅞	4 x 4⅞	4½ x 5½
D	▭	1	1½ x 2⅞	1⅞ x 3⅝	2⅛ x 4⅝	2½ x 5¼
E	▭	1	1¼ x 5⅛	1½ x 6⅝	1¾ x 8¼	2 x 9¾
F	◺	1	⅞	1	1⅛	1¼
G	▭	1	1½ x 6½	1⅞ x 8½	2⅛ x 10½	2½ x 12½
H	▲	1	1¾ x 3¾	2⅛ x 4¾	2½ x 5¾	3 x 7
I	▭	1	⅞ x 1½	1 x 1⅞	1⅛ x 2⅛	1¼ x 2½
J	◢	1	⅞ x 1¼	1 x 1½	1⅛ x 1¾	1¼ x 2
K	◥	1	2½ x 5	3⅛ x 6⅜	4 x 8	4½ x 9½
Wheel and hub cap ⚫⚪		1*, 1*	See page 10			

*Fuse on after sewing the complete block.

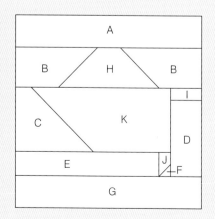

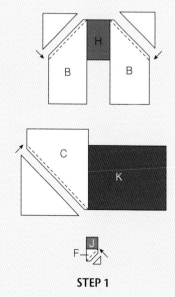

STEP 1

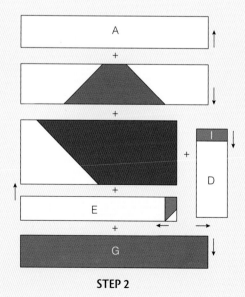

STEP 2

quilt map projects

Included in this section are ten wonderful Quilt Maps. You may pick and choose the blocks you want to use for each Map. The possibilities are endless.

Yardage and cutting charts are provided with each Quilt Map. I've overestimated the yardage needed to allow for preshrinking the fabric, squaring up, and so on. Also, I allowed 3" for the width of the binding even though I usually use 2⅛" for a double binding. Borders for Quilt Maps #3, #4, #5, #6, #7, #9, and #10 are cut longer than needed and should be trimmed to fit. The backing is 4" larger than the size of the wallhanging. These extra allowances will ensure you do not run short of fabric.

granny's cupboard

Made and quilted by Nancy Johnson-Srebro.

I enjoyed working on this wallhanging because
I was able to use many different fabrics to create
the antique-looking blocks in this old time cupboard.
Use wood-grain fabric for your pantry cupboard and
stock it with your favorite blocks!

Quilt Map #1 was used with
6" Cherry Basket (page 23)
6" Gabby the Goose (page 38)
6" Coffee Mug (page 31)
6" Basket (page 26)
6" Pineapple (page 60)
8" Antique Bottle and Crock (page 14)
8" Hurricane Lamp (page 49)
10" Classic Jug (page 27)

QUILT MAP #1

Finished Quilt Size: 37" x 39"
Finished Block Sizes: 6", 8", and 10"
Total Blocks Needed: 8

Yardage Chart (Based on 40" fabric)

Yardage for the actual blocks is not included.

Item	Quantity to Buy
A & B	⅛ YARD
*C, *D, *E, *F, G, *H & *I	1⅛ YARDS
**J, **K, **L, **M & **Binding	1¼ YARDS
Backing	41" X 43"

*Based on cutting lengthwise grain of the fabric.
**Based on cutting crosswise grain of the fabric.

Cutting Chart

Item	Cut Size	# To Cut
A	1½" x 10½"	2
B	2½" x 6½"	1
C	2" x 12½"	2
D	2" x 8½"	2
E	2" x 25½"	1
F	3" x 22"	1
G	3½" x 3½"	2
H	3" x 34"	2
I	3½" x 35½"	1
J	3½" x 4¼"	2
K	5½" x 34"	2
L	6" x 22"	1
M	3" x 37"	1

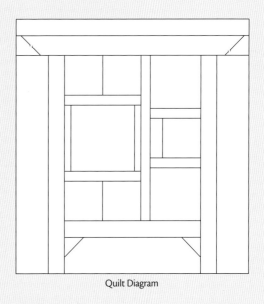

Quilt Diagram

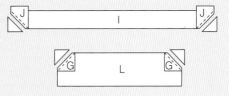

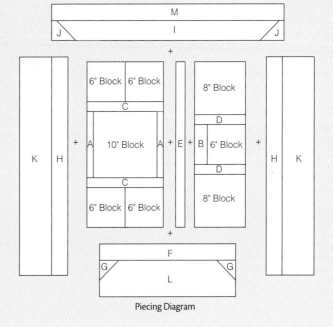

Piecing Diagram

nature's bounty

Made and quilted by Nancy Johnson-Srebro.

You can easily make this wallhanging in a weekend. Choosing the
different fabrics was more time consuming than stitching the
quilt together! You may use the same background fabric for all
four blocks or try using one fabric in four different colors.

Quilt Map #2 was used with
10" Strawberry (page 78)
10" Pear (page 80)
10" Pineapple (page 60)
10" Apple (page 30)

Finished Quilt Size: 29" x 29"
Finished Block Sizes: 10"
Total Blocks Needed: 4

Yardage Chart (Based on 40" fabric)

Yardage for the actual blocks is not included.

Item	Quantity to Buy
A	4″ X 15″ STRIP
B	4″ X 15″ STRIP
C	4″ X 15″ STRIP
D	4″ X 15″ STRIP
E, *F & *G	¾ YARD
*H & *Binding	½ YARD
Backing	33″ X 33″

*Based on cutting crosswise grain of the fabric.

Cutting Chart

Item	Cut Size	# To Cut
A	2½″ x 2½″	5
B	2½″ x 2½″	5
C	2½″ x 2½″	5
D	2½″ x 2½″	5
E	4¾″ x 4¾″	4
F	1¼″ x 40″	3
G	3½″ x 40″	3
H	1″ x 40″	3

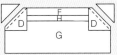

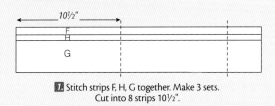

1. Stitch strips F, H, G together. Make 3 sets. Cut into 8 strips 10½".

2. Stitch the A, B, C, or D squares on the 10½" strips as shown in diagram.

3. Stitch the A, B, C, or D squares on the E square as shown in diagram.

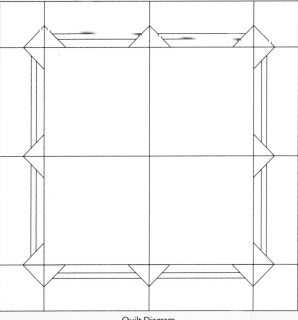

Quilt Diagram

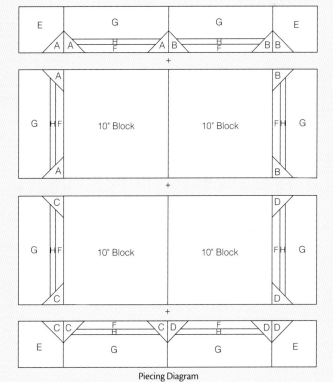

Piecing Diagram

in my neck of the woods

Made by Nancy Johnson-Srebro. Quilted by Lea Wang.

Working on this wallhanging brought back childhood memories of walking over the hill on Sundays to visit my grandmother's farm. The picket fence gives a wonderful country look to this wallhanging.

Quilt Map #3 was used with
6" Miss Lady Bug (page 57)
6" Black-eyed Susan (page 22)
6" Fancy Petunias (page 34)
6" Little Red Wagon (page 53)
6" Wheelbarrow (page 88)
9" Maple Tree (page 81)
9" High Flyer (page 40)
15" Farm House (page 52)

QUILT MAP #3

Finished Quilt Size: 40" x 42½"
Finished Block Sizes: 6", 9", and 15"
Total Blocks Needed: 10

Yardage Chart (Based on 40" fabric)

Yardage for the actual blocks is not included.

Item	Quantity to Buy
A, B, C, D, E, & F	⅜ YARD
G, H, & I	⅜ YARD
J	⅛ YARD
*Borders & *Binding	1½ YARDS
Backing	44″ X 47″

*Based on cutting crosswise grain of the fabric. You need to piece the top/bottom borders to get the length required.

Cutting Chart

Item	Cut Size	# To Cut
A	2″ x 6½″	6
B	1½″ x 33½″	1
C	2″ x 4¼″	6
D	2″ x 2¾″	6
E	2″ x 2″	8
F	1¼″ x 1¼″	32
G	1½″ x 2″	6
H	2″ x 7½″	8
I	2″ x 6″	8
J	2″ x 33½″	1
Side Borders	5″ x 33″	2
Top/Bottom Borders	5″ x 23″	4

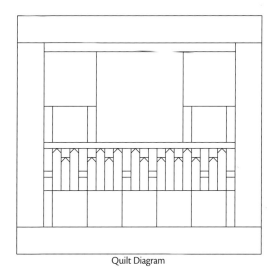

Quilt Diagram

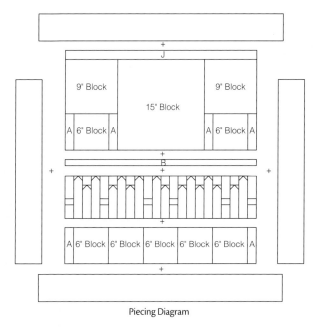

Piecing Diagram

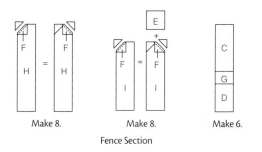

Make 8.   Make 8.   Make 6.

Fence Section

magic pillow

Made and quilted by Nancy Johnson-Srebro.

You can easily make a striking pillow in your favorite size. Mix and match 6" and 12" blocks to suit your fancy. By adjusting the width of the borders, you can make four different size pillows!

Quilt Map #4 was used with
6" Bernie the Bumblebee (page 39)
12" Fancy Petunias (page 34)
for the 24" pillow;
6" Bluebird (page 24)
12" Bird Condo (page 19)
for the 26" pillow

Finished Pillow Size: Varies from 18" to 26"
Finished Block Sizes: 6" and 12"
Total Blocks Needed: 2

Yardage Chart (Based on 40" fabric)
Yardage for the actual blocks is not included.

Item	Quantity to Buy
A for 18" Pillow	8" X 15" STRIP
A and *Borders for 22" Pillow	½ YARD
A and *Borders for 24" Pillow	⅝ YARD
A and *Borders for 26" Pillow	¾ YARD
B	8" X 15" STRIP
Backing for 18" Pillow	⅝ YARD
Backing for 22" Pillow	¾ YARD
Backing for 24" Pillow	¾ YARD
Backing for 26" Pillow	⅞ YARD

*Based on cutting crosswise grain of the fabric.

Cutting Chart

Item	Cut Size	# To Cut
**A	6½" x 6½"	2
**B	6½" x 6½"	2
18" Pillow		
Backing	13" x 18½"	2
22" Pillow		
Side Borders	2½" x 20"	2
Top/Bottom Borders	2½" x 24"	2
Backing	15" x 22½"	2
24" Pillow		
Side Borders	3½" x 20"	2
Top/Bottom Borders	3½" x 26"	2
Backing	16" x 24½"	2
26" Pillow		
Side Borders	4½" x 20"	2
Top/Bottom Borders	4½" x 28"	2
Backing	17" x 26½"	2

**Cut each square in half diagonally once to make two triangles.

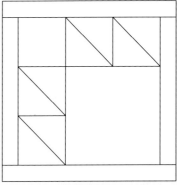

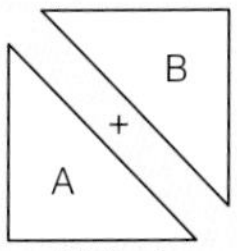

Quilt Diagram

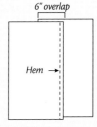

6" overlap

Make 4.

Hem →

1. Hem the inner edges of the two backing panels using a ¾" seam allowance.
2. Overlap the two backing pieces by 6". Depending on the pillow size, the backing piece will now measure either 18½" square, 22½" square, 24½" square, or 26½" square.
3. With right sides together, stitch the pillow front to the pillow back. Turn the pillow covering right side out. Insert the pillow form.

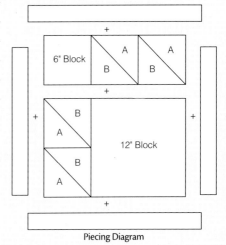

Piecing Diagram

summer sailing

Made by Nancy Johnson-Srebro. Quilted by Lea Wang.

This is one of my favorite wallhangings. I like the scene above and below the water. To make the quilt flow together, I only used one fish in the Swimmin' Fish blocks and then filled in with extra fabric. Have fun choosing fabric for the water and sky.

Quilt Map #5 was used with
6" Sea Turtle (page 44)
6" Swimmin' Fish (page 69)
9" Lighthouse (page 84)
12" Sails a'Flying (page 12)

QUILT MAP #5

Finished Quilt Size: 31¾" x 40"
Finished Block Sizes: 6", 9", and 12"
Total Blocks Needed: 6

Yardage Chart (Based on 40" fabric)

Yardage for the actual blocks is not included.

Item	Quantity to Buy
A, B, C, D, E	⅜ YARD
F	4″ X 10″ STRIP
G, H, I, J	¼ YARD
*Inner Borders	¼ YARD
*Outer Borders & *Binding	1¼ YARDS
Backing	36″ X 44″

*Based on cutting crosswise grain of the fabric. You need to piece the top/bottom borders to get the length required.

Cutting Chart

Item	Cut Size	# To Cut
A	2½″ x 9½″	1
B	5¾″ x 23″	1
C	2¾″ x 2¾″	1
D	5½″ x 9″	1
E	6″ x 9″	1
F	3¼″ x 9½″	1
G	4″ x 6″	2
**H	5⅛″ x 5⅛″	2
I	5½″ x 6½″	1
J	1½″ x 9″	1
Inner Side Borders	1½″ x 25″	2
Inner Top/Bottom Borders	1½″ x 35″	2
Outer Side Borders	3½″ x 27″	2
Outer Top/Bottom Borders	3½″ x 22″	4

**Cut each square in half diagonally once to make two triangles. ◨

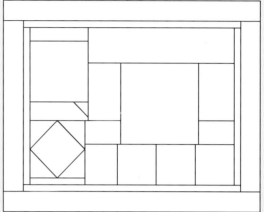

Quilt Diagram

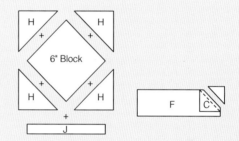

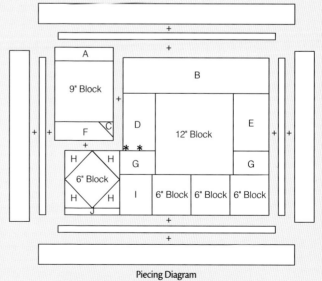

Piecing Diagram

Don't sew between the ✱. Add the 9" block unit to B/D unit, then finish sewing the F/H/D/G seam closed.

christmas time!

Made by Nancy Johnson-Srebro. Quilted by Lea Wang.

Rudolph had to be part of this Christmas quilt but he was a 9" block instead of 10". To make this block 10", I increased the unfinished width of the A and C pieces by ½" and added a 1½" unfinished strip along the bottom of the block. To make a memory quilt, have your family and friends sign their names on the star points.

Quilt Map #6 was used with
6" Snowflakes (page 64)
9" Rudolph (page 86)
10" Stockings for Everyone (page 61)
10" Mr. Frosty (page 35)
10" All Tied Up (page 68)
15" Saint Nick (page 28)

QUILT MAP #6

Finished Quilt Size: 48½" x 48½"
Finished Block Sizes: 6", 10" and 15"
Total Blocks Needed: 9

Yardage Chart (Based on 40" fabric)
Yardage for the actual blocks is not included.

Item	Quantity to Buy
A	½ YARD
*B, *C, *D, *E	1¼ YARDS
**Borders & **Binding	1½ YARDS
Backing	53" x 53"

*Based on cutting crosswise grain of the fabric.
**Based on cutting lengthwise grain of the fabric.

Cutting Chart

Item	Cut Size	# To Cut
A	8" x 8"	8
B	2¼" x 10½"	8
C	2¼" x 14"	8
D	6½" x 9½"	4
E	8" x 15½"	4
Side Borders	3½" x 44"	2
Top/Bottom Borders	3½" x 50"	2

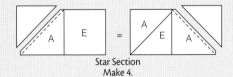

Star Section
Make 4.

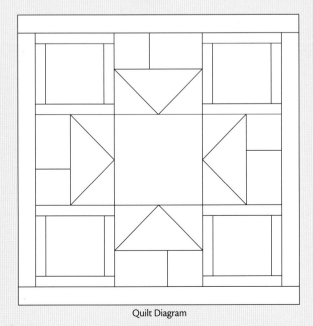

Quilt Diagram

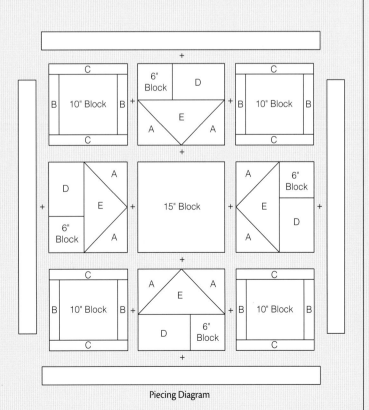

Piecing Diagram

Quilt Map #7 was used with
6" Moon Rockets (page 56)
15" Uncle Sam (page 70)

freedom

Made by Nancy Johnson-Srebro. Quilted by Lea Wang.

I named this wallhanging "Freedom" because of
the two powerful symbols of our independence
and progress. This is a quick and easy day project!
This setting will showcase any 15" block. His face
is embellished with a mustache and eyes.

QUILT MAP #7

Finished Quilt Size: 29" x 29"
Finished Block Sizes: 6" and 15"
Total Blocks Needed: 5

Yardage Chart (Based on 40" fabric)
Yardage for the actual blocks is not included.

Item	Quantity to Buy
*A, *Borders, & *Binding	¾ YARD
*B	¼ YARD
*C	¼ YARD
Backing	33" X 33"

*Based on cutting crosswise grain of the fabric.

Cutting Chart

Item	Cut Size	# To Cut
A	2½" x 15½"	4
B	2½" x 15½"	4
C	2½" x 15½"	4
Side Borders	1¼" x 29"	2
Top/Bottom Borders	1¼" x 31"	2

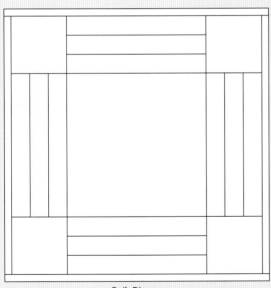

Quilt Diagram

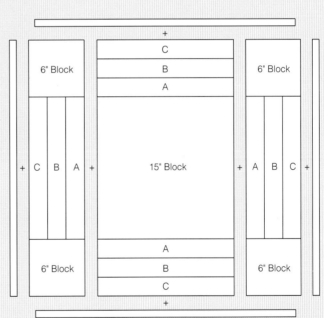

Piecing Diagram

Quilt Map #8 was used with
4" and 6" Shooting Stars (page 65)
4" and 6" Double Hearts (page 11)
6" Tom the Turkey (page 20)
6" Heart to Hearts (page 42)
6" Cardinal (page 32)
6" and 12" Log Cabins (page 66)
6" and 12" Farm Houses (page 52)
6" and 12" Barney the Bears (page 16)
6" and 12" Mikey Mooses (page 74)
6", 6" x 12", 12" Twin Pines (page 54)

into the woods

Made by Maryjane Simpson. Quilted by Leslie Armando.

This map is so user-friendly you could easily make many different
size wallhangings by stitching only the sections that you want.
Maryjane's comments: Doesn't this look like a great outdoor
adventure? My husband has claimed the quilt as "his!"

Finished Quilt Size: 64½" x 80½"
Finished Block Sizes: 4", 6", 6" x 12", 12"
Total Blocks Needed: 35

Yardage Chart (Based on 40" fabric)
Yardage for the actual blocks is not included.

Item	Quantity to Buy
A	(16) 4″ x 8½″ STRIPS OF VARIOUS SCRAPS
B	(16) 5″ SQUARES OF VARIOUS SCRAPS
C	(60) 3″ SQUARES OF VARIOUS SCRAPS
D	(132) 3″ x 7″ STRIPS OF VARIOUS SCRAPS
*Inner Borders	¾ YARD
*Binding	⅞ YARD
Backing	69″ x 85″

*Based on cutting crosswise grain of fabric. You need to piece the border to get the required length.

Cutting Chart

Item	Cut Size	# To Cut
**A	3⅞″ x 3⅞″	32
B	4¾″ x 4¾″	16
C	2½″ x 2½″	60
D	2½″ x 6½″	132
Inner Side Borders	2½″ x 34″	4
Inner Top/Bottom Borders	2½″ x 28″	4

**Cut each square in half diagonally once to make two triangles.

Make 16.

Count on the diagram, how many C pieces to stitch together for each strip.

Stitch 2 strips of 26 D for the top and bottom borders.
Stitch 2 strips of 40 D for the side borders.

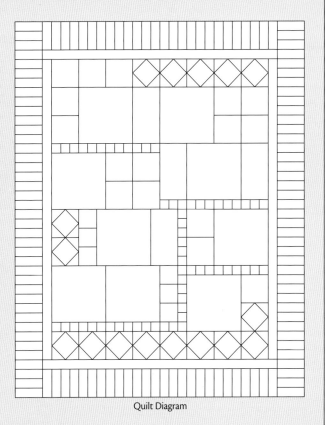

Quilt Diagram

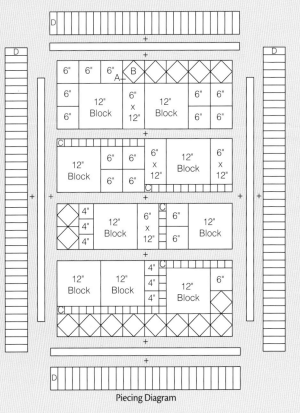

Piecing Diagram

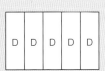

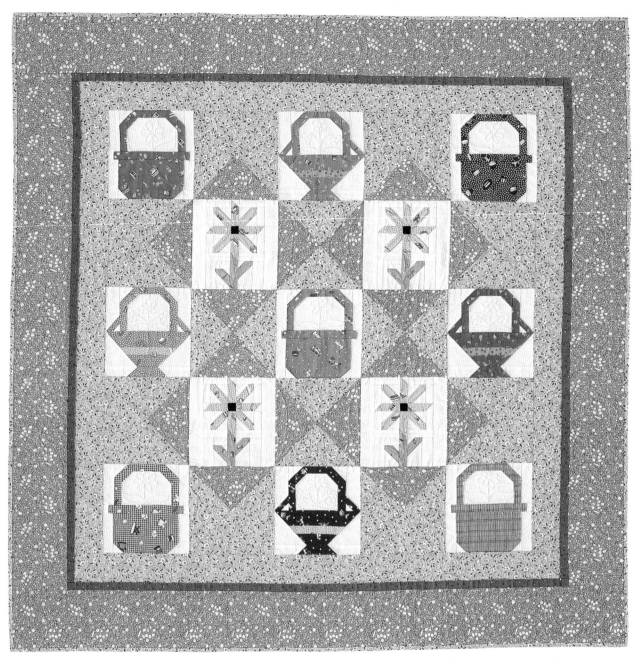

Quilt Map #9 was used with
6" Cherry Baskets (page 23)
6" Baskets (page 26)
6" Black-eyed Susans (page 22)

arlene's baskets!

Made by C.A. Warner-Bradigan. Quilted by Mary Schilke.

This map allows the outside blocks to appear as if

they are floating!

C.A.'s comments: Baskets have been a favorite pattern

of quilters throughout the years. Try this quilt in

reproduction fabrics or plaids for a different look.

Finished Quilt Size: 44½" x 44½"
Finished Block Sizes: 6"
Total Blocks Needed: 13

Yardage Chart (Based on 40" fabric)
Yardage for the actual blocks is not included.

Item	Quantity to Buy
A, B & *Inner Borders	⅞ YARD
C, *Outer Borders	1¼ YARDS
*Middle Borders	¼ YARD
*Binding	½ YARD
Backing	49" X 49"

*Based on cutting crosswise grain of the fabric. You need to piece the top/bottom outer borders to get the required length.

Cutting Chart

Item	Cut Size	# To Cut
**A	6⅞" x 6⅞"	4
***B	7¼" x 7¼"	4
***C	7¼" x 7¼"	4
Inner Borders	2½" x 36"	4
Middle Border	1½" x 38"	4
Side Outer Borderes	4½" x 40"	2
Top/Bottom Outer Borders	4½" x 25"	4

**Cut each square in half diagonally once to make two triangles. ◲
***Cut each square in half diagonally twice to make four triangles. ⊠

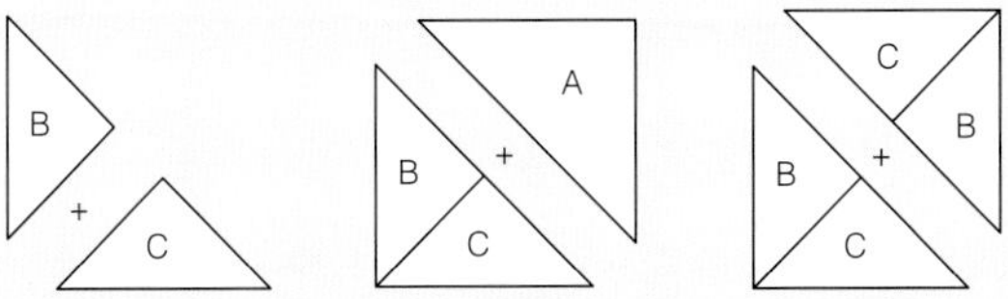

Make 16.

Make 8.

Make 4.

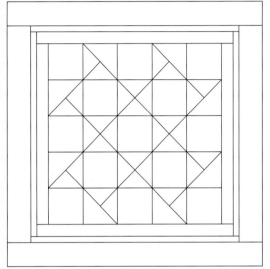

Quilt Diagram

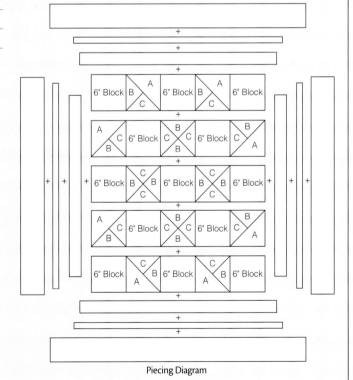

Piecing Diagram

victorian birthday

Made and quilted by Janet McCarroll.

This table runner is so quick and easy you'll want to make one for every season.
Janet's comments: Surprise someone on their birthday with a table runner made especially for the occasion. Make it a tradition to use it every year afterward.

Quilt Map #10 was used with 12" Happy Birthday Cakes! (page 43).

QUILT MAP #10

Finished Quilt Size: 20½" x 52½"
Finished Block Size: 12"
Total Blocks Needed: 2

Yardage Chart (Based on 40" fabric)
Yardage for the actual blocks is not included.

Item	Quantity to Buy
*A & *E	½ YARD
B	6½" SQUARE
C	5¼" X 11" STRIP
D	(8) 5¼" SQUARES OF VARIOUS SCRAPS
*Borders & *Binding	1 YARD
Backing	25" X 57"

*Based on cutting crosswise grain of the fabric.

Cutting Chart

Item	Cut Size	# To Cut
A	2½" X 12½"	4
B	6⅛" X 6⅛"	1
**C	4⅞" X 4⅞"	2
**D	4⅞" X 4⅞"	8
E	4½" X 24½"	2
Side Borders	2½" X 26"	4
Top/Bottom Borders	2½" X 23"	2

**Cut each square in half diagonally once to make two triangles.

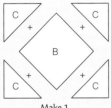

Make 1.

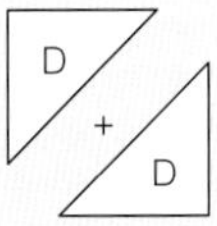

Make 8. 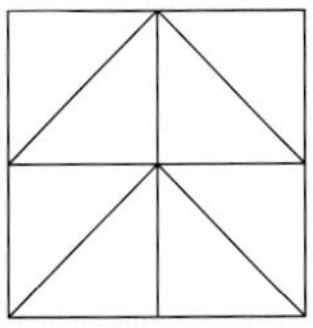   Make 2 sets.

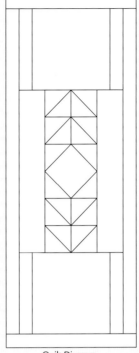

Quilt Diagram

Piecing Diagram

RESOURCES

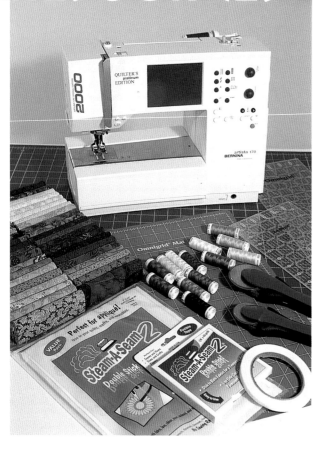

■ **American & Efird, Inc.**
Consumer Products Division
24 American St.
Mt. Holly, NC 28120
www.amefird.com

■ **Benartex, Inc.**
1359 Broadway, Suite 1100
New York, NY 10018
www.benartex.com

■ **Bernina of America**
3500 Thayer Ct.
Aurora, IL 60504
www.berninausa.com

■ **Fairfield Processing Corporation**
P. O. Box 1157
Danbury, CT 06813
www.poly-fil.com

■ **FreeSpirit**
1350 Broadway, 21st Floor
New York, NY 10018
www.freespiritfabric.com

■ **Just Another Button Company**
116 West Market Street
Troy, IL 62294
(wholesale only)
(618) 667-8531

■ **P&B Textiles**
1580 Gilbreth Road
Burlingame, CA 94010
www.pbtex.com

■ **Prym Dritz/Omnigrid**
P. O. Box 5028
Spartanburg, SC 29304
www.dritz.com

■ **RJR Fashion Fabrics**
13748 S. Gramercy Place
Gardena, CA 90249
www.rjrfabrics.com

■ **Robert Kaufman Co., Inc.**
129 W. 132nd Street
Los Angeles, CA 90061
www.robertkaufman.com

■ **Stearns Technical Textiles Company**
100 Williams Street
Cincinnati, OH 45215
www.stearnstextiles.com

■ **Timeless Treasures**
483 Broadway
New York, NY 10013
www.ttfabrics.com

■ **The Warm Company**
954 East Union Street
Seattle, WA 98122
www.warmcompany.com

about the author

Nancy is highly sought after as a quilt-piecing designer, teacher, lecturer, and show judge. She has developed No-Fail® methods for accurate rotary cutting and machine piecing. She's also refined how to select and use different size blocks for larger projects with her leading-edge Quilt Map® concept.

She has been a spokesperson for Omnigrid, a division of Prym Dritz, for over 12 years.

Nancy has written several best sellers including *Featherweight 221—The Perfect Portable®*, *Measure the Possibilities with Omnigrid*, *Endless Possibilities*, *Rotary Magic*, and *Block Magic*.

Nancy lives in Pennsylvania with her husband, Frank. They have three grown children and one granddaughter. She travels extensively to teach and lecture on the wonderful art of quiltmaking.

OTHER FINE BOOKS FROM C&T PUBLISHING

On the Surface: Thread Embellishment & Fabric Manipulation, Wendy Hill

Paper Piecing Picnic: Fun-Filled Projects for Every Quilter, From the Editors and Contributors of Quilter's Newsletter Magazine and Quiltmaker Magazine

Paper Piecing Potpourri: Fun-Filled Projects for Every Quilter, Quilter's Newsletter magazine & Quiltmaker Magazine

Paper Piecing with Alex Anderson: •Tips •Techniques •6 Projects, Alex Anderson

Patchwork Persuasion: Fascinating Quilts from Traditional Designs, Joen Wolfrom

Patchwork Quilts Made Easy - Revised, 2nd Edition: 33 Quilt Favorites, Old & New, Jean Wells

Perfect Union of Patchwork & Appliqué, A, Darlene Christopherson

Photo Transfer Handbook, The: Snap It, Print It, Stitch It!, Jean Ray Laury

Pieced Clothing Variations, Yvonne Porcella

Pieced Flowers, Ruth B. McDowell

Pieced Roman Shades, Terrell Sundermann

Pieced Vegetables, Ruth B. McDowell

Piecing: Expanding the Basics, Ruth B. McDowell

Provence Quilts and Cuisine, Marie-Christine Flocard & Cosabeth Parriaud

Q is for Quilt, Diana McClun & Laura Nownes

Quick Quilts for the Holidays: 11 Projects to Stamp, Stencil, and Sew, Trice Boerens

Quilt It for Kids: 11 Projects, Sports, Animal, Fantasy Themes, For Children of All Ages, Pam Bono

Quilted Garden, The: Design & Make Nature-Inspired Quilts, Jane Sassaman

Quilting Back to Front: Fun & Easy No-Mark Techniques, Larraine Scouler

Quilting with Carol Armstrong: •30 Quilting Patterns•Appliqué Designs•16 Projects, Carol Armstrong

Quilting with the Muppets: 15 Fun and Creative Projects, The Jim Henson Company in association with the Sesame Workshop

Quilts for Guys: 15 Fun Projects For Your Favorite Fella, Compilation

Quilts from the Civil War: Nine Projects, Historic Notes, Diary Entries, Barbara Brackman

Quilts, Quilts, and More Quilts!, Diana McClun & Laura Nownes

Ultimate Guide to Longarm Quilting, The: •How to Use Any Longarm Machine •Techniques, Patterns & Pantographs •Starting a Business •Hiring a Longarm Machine Quilter, Linda Taylor

Radiant New York Beauties: 14 Paper-Pieced Quilt Projects, Valori Wells

Rag Wool Appliqué: •Easy to Sew •Use Any Sewing Machine •Quilts, Home Decor & Clothing, Kathy MacMannis

Reverse Appliqué with No Brakez, Jan Mullen

Rotary Cutting with Alex Anderson: Tips, Techniques, and Projects, Alex Anderson

Rx for Quilters: Stitcher-Friendly Advice for Every Body, Susan Delaney-Mech

Say It with Quilts, Diana McClun & Laura Nownes

Scrap Quilts: The Art of Making Do, Roberta Horton

Setting Solutions, Sharyn Craig

Sew Much Fun: 14 Projects to Stitch & Embroider, Oklahoma Embroidery Supply & Design

Shadow Quilts, Patricia Magaret & Donna Slusser

Shadow Redwork™ with Alex Anderson: 24 Designs to Mix and Match, Alex Anderson

Shoreline Quilts: Glorious Get-Away Projects, compiled by Cyndy Lyle Rymer

Show Me How to Machine Quilt: A Fun, No-Mark Approach, Kathy Sandbach

Simple Fabric Folding for Christmas: 14 Festive Quilts & Projects, Liz Aneloski

Simply Stars: Quilts That Sparkle, Alex Anderson

Skydyes: A Visual Guide to Fabric Painting, Mickey Lawler

Slice of Christmas from Piece O' Cake Designs, A, Linda Jenkins & Becky Goldsmith

Small Scale Quiltmaking: Precision, Proportion, and Detail, Sally Collins

Smashing Sets: Exciting Ways to Arrange Quilt Blocks, Margaret J. Miller

Snowflakes & Quilts, Paula Nadelstern

Soft-Edge Piecing: Add the Elegance of Appliqué to Traditional-Style Patchwork Design, Jinny Beyer

Special Delivery Quilts, Patrick Lose

Start Quilting with Alex Anderson, 2nd Edition: Six Projects for First-Time Quilters, Alex Anderson

Stitch 'n Flip Quilts : 14 Fantastic Projects, Valori Wells

Stripes In Quilts, Mary Mashuta

Strips 'n Curves: A New Spin on Strip Piecing, Louisa L. Smith

Thimbleberries Housewarming, A: 22 Projects for Quilters, Lynette Jensen

Through the Garden Gate: Quilters and Their Gardens, Jean & Valori Wells

Tradition with a Twist: Variations on Your Favorite Quilts, Blanche Young & Dalene Young-Stone

Trapunto by Machine, Hari Walner

Travels with Peaky and Spike: Doreen Speckmann's Quilting Adventures, Doreen Speckmann

Visual Dance, The: Creating Spectacular Quilts, Joen Wolfrom

Wild Birds: Designs for Appliqué & Quilting, Carol Armstrong

Wildflowers: Designs for Appliqué and Quilting, Carol Armstrong

Wine Country Quilts: A Bounty of Flavorful Projects for Any Palette, Cyndy Lyle Rymer and Jennifer Rounds

Workshop with Velda Newman, A: Adding Dimension to Your Quilts, Velda E. Newman

Yvonne Porcella: Art & Inspirations:, Yvonne Porcella

For more information write for a free catalog:
C&T Publishing, Inc.
P.O. Box 1456
Lafayette, CA 94549
(800) 284-1114
E-mail: ctinfo@ctpub.com
Website: www.ctpub.com

For quilting supplies:
Cotton Patch Mail Order
3405 Hall Lane, Dept.CTB
Lafayette, CA 94549
(800) 835-4418
(925) 283-7883
E-mail:quiltusa@yahoo.com
Website: www.quiltusa.com

Note:
Fabrics used in the quilts shown may not be currently available since fabric manufacturers keep most fabrics in print for only a short time.